HAS GOD *REALLY* FINISHED
WITH ISRAEL?

HAS GOD *REALLY* FINISHED WITH ISRAEL?

GOD'S COVENANTS WITH ABRAHAM, ISRAEL AND THE CHURCH

Mark Dunman

New Wine Press

New Wine Press

An imprint of
Roperpenberthy Publishing Ltd
Springfield House
23 Oatlands Drive
Weybridge KY13 9LZ
United Kingdom

ISBN 978-1-905991-87-7

Typeset by **documen**, www.documen.co.uk
Printed in the United Kingdom

CONTENTS

MAPS

FOREWORD

Mark Dunman is not a professional theologian or writer and so his book is a refreshing and thought-provoking challenge to many readers. It covers a range of issues touching the debate about land borders and the use of biblical prophecy and gives solid biblical grounds for supporting the restoration of the Jewish people to the land of Israel.

For those who are familiar with the writings of those who promote what is generally termed Replacement Theology, many of whom also deny the validity of Israel's restoration, he gives a firm and uncompromising challenge. For others who are new to these issues there are clear-cut biblical issues to chew upon. Happily he avoids the prophetic dogmatism of some writers in this field.

Mark has demonstrated his integrity in seeking to understand the Palestinian Christian perspective by spending time with Palestinian Christians in the West Bank and seeing first-hand the very real problems they live with day by day, not least because of the restrictions in movement they experience because of the security wall and checkpoints. In fact I personally recently spent time with him at such a conference in Bethlehem and noted his willingness to listen and understand that local situation, and his encouragement to both sides to engage with each other without preconditions.

At the same time he takes issue with Palestinian Liberation Theology which is proving a real barrier to Western Christians relating positively to Israel. He has listened well and understood.

Having personally spent very much time visiting Israel and also getting to know Palestinian Christians in the West Bank including living among them from time to time, I know how complex this situation is. Woe betide us if we take a narrow one or two-dimensional view of Israel today either politically or biblically. In every way the Israeli/Palestinian situation is multi-dimensional and complex, and the only way forward is the way of Christ who walked through all the barriers in the turbulent society of his day, and brought the grace of God into people's lives.

When we have studied and sought to understand, our response must be to pray, and in particular, support the believing body in the land whether Jew or Palestinian or of whatever background. That is Mark's closing challenge.

Derek White
Founder and former Director of Christian Friends of Israel UK
March 2013

PREFACE

This book is born of a desire to encourage Christians to recognise God's prophetic return of the Jewish people to the land of Israel and to alert the Church at large to the need to pray for Israel, the Jewish people, the Palestinians and the whole complex situation in the Middle East.

It is intended for Christians who want to know more about Israel and what the scriptures have to say about it. There is a debate in the Church about the place of Israel in the modern world. There are those who believe the return of the Jews is a fulfilment of Bible prophecy – this book is firmly on their side; and there are those who believe Israel is simply another secular state, with little, if any, biblical significance.

There are many scriptures which support the return of the Jews to the Holy Land and this book makes use of a great many of them. It also confronts head-on the arguments of those writers and theologians who are opposed to this view. It deals comprehensively with the objections they make to the view that modern-day Israel is significant in God's purposes.

It is not a book about the politics of the Middle East, about whether we should side with the Jews in Israel or the Palestinians in the West Bank and Gaza. I have been to Israel and to the West Bank and read widely on the subject. It becomes a hopeless task to sort out the rights and wrongs on the basis of politics alone. The history of Palestine/ Israel over the last 130 years is too complex to arrive at a balanced view from a purely human angle.

However, it is possible to arrive at a conclusion based on God's Word as given to us in the Bible. This is the conclusion that God is fulfilling his promise to the Jews to restore them to their ancient land

and that as Christians we need to support this. This does not mean that Israel's policies and actions are always right, or that they have handled their relationship with the Palestinians correctly, or that God thinks they have done so. Israel has sometimes got it wrong; but if that is true of Israel, it is also true of the surrounding Arab nations and the Palestinian leadership.

I originally planned to include a section entitled "Israel's Recent History", but after much reflection I decided against this. Instead I have used my opening chapter to give a flavour of the political debate which surrounds Israel, by presenting opposing perceptions. This sometimes helps one to see the situation from both sides. I have touched on the history in Chapter 3, *Has God been asleep for the last 130 years?* and I have also presented an historical timeline on the associated website. This is principally to help readers who may be new to the debate about Israel. There are good books available on the history and politics of the Middle East and some of these are listed in the bibliography.

One important fact that we do need to recognise is that large numbers of Jews and Palestinian Arabs now live in Palestine/Israel. Both sides claim a right to live there on account of their historical connection to the land, the Jews by right of their ancient connection to the land, and the Palestinians by right of a more recent connection. In the last two millennia, both Jewish and Palestinian families have lived in the land for centuries.

This book is a wake-up call to the Church because the Middle East conflict has led to a denial of Israel's right to be in the land. The underlying argument for Christians to hold this view has been a re-interpretation of what the scriptures have to say about Israel and the return of the Jews. This theology appeared early in Church history and has re-appeared in the twentieth century. It appears under various names, but is most commonly known as 'Replacement Theology'. It serves to undermine the biblical restoration of Israel and to make it nothing more that a twentieth century secular state.

This theology is wrong. It is an unwarranted interpretation of what the Old Testament actually says about Israel and the Jews and a principal purpose of this book is to demonstrate this. It is difficult to avoid the conclusion that for many Christians acceptance of replacement theology has been motivated by their perception of Israel's behaviour towards the Palestinians. It is easier for a Christian to feel negative towards Israel if Israel is no longer part of God's purpose on the earth. I cannot overemphasise that this approach is the wrong way round. We have to be single-minded about the meaning of the Bible, its Covenants and Old Testament promises. We cannot determine theology only by reference to perceived behaviour.

It is still possible to feel critical of Israel while recognising its biblical right to be in the land. I am not alone among supporters of Israel in being critical of some of its policies and actions and of the suffering of ordinary Palestinians in their daily lives in the West Bank. However, it does mean that one examines Israel's behaviour in the historical context of the last century. One asks why the Jews and later the State of Israel have taken a particular course of action. One cannot ignore the hostility of the surrounding Arab nations, the Palestinian leaders or the present leaders of Iran and criticize Israel's behaviour in a vacuum.

For those who are new to the debate, but wondering about Israel in the midst of conflicting views, I hope they will be persuaded by my arguments from the Bible that God has been restoring the Jews to their ancient homeland and the rebirth of the State of Israel is a part of this.

The last chapter is devoted to the subject of praying for Israel and the Middle East. I believe that this is really important to God; that he calls the Church to partner with him in achieving his purposes on earth. We can do this with much more conviction if we have a clear view of God's purpose for Israel and the Jewish people. If we think that Israel is merely another secular nation, then we are less likely to want to pray for them. If our hearts are open to the Holy Spirit, then ultimately God will lead us to pray as he wishes. This could be for Israel and the Jews or it could be for the Palestinians, or it could be for other aspects of the situation in the Middle East. We can then be confident that we are praying according to his purposes (1 John 5:14-15).

I have already introduced a number of terms which may be unfamiliar to readers. It is my hope that the book will serve as a reference book as well as a narrative. I have therefore included the following: appendices, glossary, bibliography, index of Scripture references and general index. However, in order to keep the book to a manageable size I have assigned all of these to the following website: <*www.markdunman. com*>. Reference to a website is becoming more common with authors.

I would encourage the reader to access this website and in particular to read the first two appendices: *Covenantalists' Objections to Christian Zionism* and *Covenantalists under the Spotlight*. The first deals with verses in the New Testament which are raised as objections to the theme of this book, while the second deals in detail with the weaknesses in the arguments of those who support replacement theology.

A word on sources is appropriate. These days the World Wide Web is a wonderful source of information and is increasingly used as a reference source by authors. I have made considerable use of the Internet encyclopaedia, Wikipedia, in my notes.. It is easy to access and avoids detailed web addresses. Newspaper or journal articles cited in the notes can mostly be found on-line. These web addresses were all accessible as of December 2012. I have tried to avoid more remote web articles, which may get withdrawn. Where this has happened a Google search will usually display alternative websites. Out of print books can often be obtained through on-line bookshops such as Amazon.

Scripture quotations are taken from the English Standard Version (ESV) and occasionally as indicated, from the Revised Standard Version (RSV) or the New International Version (NIV). For dates I have used the more traditional BC and AD (Before Christ and Anno Domini) rather than the modern BCE and CE (Before Common Era and Common Era). In chapters where I have quoted more than a few Scriptures, I have numbered the scriptures for easy reference within each chapter.

I am grateful to my prayer group *Watchmen for Israel* for praying for, and encouraging me, in this endeavour. I should like to thank my two friends, Sophia and Jane, for allowing me to share the stories of how they came to pray for Israel and the Jewish people in Chapters 2 and 12 respectively. I am grateful to Derek White and other friends for reading the manuscript and suggesting changes and also to my publisher for his professional help.

I am especially grateful to my wife, Margaret, for her down to earth wisdom, encouraging me to stick to a deadline and not least for typing the manuscript!

Mark Dunman
December 2012

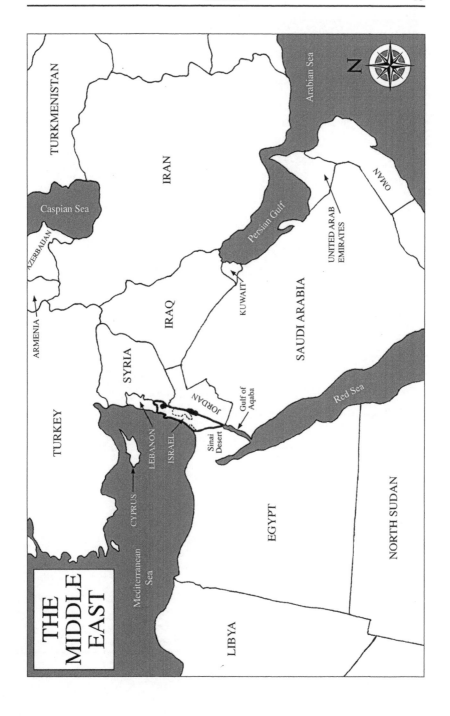

1 *OUR PERCEPTION OF ISRAEL*

The Israeli/Palestinian conflict is the most divisive conflict in the world today. Since this book is addressed to Christians it is important to state at the outset that the issue also divides Christians, and in particular evangelical Christians, into two groups – those who support Israel and those who support the Palestinians. Since the Six-Day War in 1967 an increasingly vocal group of evangelical Christians, particularly in America, have come to support Israel, because they believe they are witnessing the fulfilment of Old Testament prophecy concerning Israel and the end times (the Return of Christ). More recently, and particularly in the last ten years, other evangelical Christians have come to identify with the Palestinians whom they see as being oppressed by Israel's occupation of the West Bank. We will look briefly at the views of these two groups of Christians.

Supporters of Israel

They view the rebirth of the nation of Israel in 1948 in the Holy Land as nothing short of a miracle. They believe that this is the fulfilment of prophecy; that God promised that one day the Jewish people would be a nation once again in their ancient land.

They point out that the re-establishment of Israel as a nation has been achieved in the face of violent hostility from the surrounding Arab states. Since its rebirth in 1948 the nation and its people have known nothing but war or the need to be prepared for war. Israel's supporters point to the fact that Israel has been involved in five major wars. In these and other military engagements, including terrorist activities by their enemies, Israel has lost over 22,000 citizens, a very high figure relative to its population.[1] It has had to remain in a high state of alert to guard against invasion or terror attacks from the surrounding Arab nations and the Palestinians.

Israel's supporters also make the point that the Arab nations now have seventeen states across a large swathe of North Africa and the Middle East. No one questions the right of the Arab states to be Arab and furthermore for many of them to be strongly Muslim, and yet the Arabs argue that Israel is being racist by demanding that its state be Jewish. They argue: surely it is not asking too much of the Arab states to accept a Jewish state representing a mere 0.2% (1 in 500 parts) of the territory owned and ruled by the Arabs?[2]

Despite the state being Jewish and despite the external threats, its supporters point out that it is a vibrant democracy with 1.5 million Arabs (exceeding 20% of Israel's population). They have their own political parties and some of them reach high positions in Israeli society. They point out that Jews are not allowed to settle in neighbouring Arab territories, and that in other Arab countries there are only a tiny remnant of Jews remaining in states which had thriving Jewish communities until 1948.[3] They also add that Israel has freedom to worship: it is tolerant of other faiths unlike many of its autocratic Arab neighbours.

Supporters further point to the miraculous agricultural and later technological development of the nation. It is one of the most advanced nations in the world today. They argue that if campaigners are serious about boycotting Israeli goods, it is not enough to refuse to buy Israeli agricultural produce. They will have to discard much of their computing and phone equipment, because it is likely to contain parts developed and made in Israel.

Finally, supporters of Israel argue that it is truly amazing that despite the very real military threats which include the threat by Iran's leaders to destroy the state[4] and the ongoing rocket attacks by Hamas from Gaza,[5] Israel is still able to remain a democracy and to develop socially and economically.

Opponents of Israel

The opponents of Israel see it very differently. They regard Israel as a usurper state which has deprived the native Arabs (Palestinians) of their homeland, where many families have lived for centuries.

They discount the fact that Israel was a state in this area for over 1000 years and argue that most Jews had left the land (in exile) by AD 135. They consider that this does not entitle modern-day Jews to come back and reclaim the land nearly 2000 years later.

They further argue that the very act of establishing the nation in 1948 led to the expulsion of 750,000 Palestinians from their homes in Israel. Since then they have either lived in refugee camps, settled in the West Bank and Gaza or settled in Jordan. This number has now grown to four million and Israel has resolutely refused to allow the refugees or their descendants back into Israel.

They argue that this injustice has been compounded since the Six-Day War in 1967 by Israel's occupation of Gaza and the West Bank.[6] Israel treated the Palestinian population harshly. It was not willing to entertain an independent Palestinian state until forced to face the unpopularity of its occupation during the First Intifada in 1987.[7]

They consider that Israel compounded the injustice of the occupation by allowing Jewish settlements in the West Bank and Gaza[8] before resolving the issue of land ownership. As these settlements expanded they began to take land that had been owned or tenanted by Palestinian farmers for centuries. Unless Palestinians can show watertight ownership of the land, the Israeli authorities declare it to be state land. In other cases it can be confiscated for military purposes by order of the military governor. Some of this land then finds its way into the hands of settlers.[9]

The opponents of Israel argue that although the separation barrier (fence or wall) was initially built, starting in 2002, to prevent suicide bombings and terror attacks in Israel proper, it has since become a means of stealing Palestinian land. This is because the barrier does not follow the Green Line,[10] but branches out into the West Bank to incorporate Israel's major settlements. Where smaller and more distant settlements exist in the West Bank they are being supplied by roads and utilities that are not available to the Palestinians. The settlements are also governed by Israeli law. Thus, whether by design or accident, Israel is establishing two parallel societies in the West Bank, one for Jews and one for Palestinians. This is in Area C, the 59% of the West Bank remaining outside the autonomous areas of the Palestinian Authority now under Palestinian control.[11]

Finally, they argue that the separation barrier has become a means of punishing and humiliating the Palestinians. Until ten years ago many Palestinians crossed the Green Line to work in Israel and there was much inter-communal activity. For example, there were agricultural markets in the border towns. Most of this has ceased, and the Palestinians have been the main losers. Palestinians have difficulty in obtaining work permits and when they do have them they may have to queue for hours to pass through the checkpoints. Without the necessary permit for work, health or social reasons, permission to cross the border is refused.

Israel's challenge to this narrative

It is only fair to say that Israel would challenge this hostile narrative at a number of points.

They would argue that at each crisis point they have been defending their right to exist as a nation and are still having to do this today. They would quote Prime Minister Binyamin Netanyahu from a speech in 2006:

> The truth is that if Israel were to put down its arms there
> would be no more Israel. If the Arabs were to put down their
> arms, there would be no more war.[12]

They would argue that the Palestinians could have had a state in 1948 if the Arab nations had accepted the United Nations partition plan. This was voted for on 29 November 1947.[13] Instead, they argue, the Palestinians reacted violently the next day, ambushing and killing Jews travelling by bus. This quickly let to civil war. This was later followed by the invasion by five Arab states once the British had given up the mandate for Palestine and left on 14 May 1948.[14]

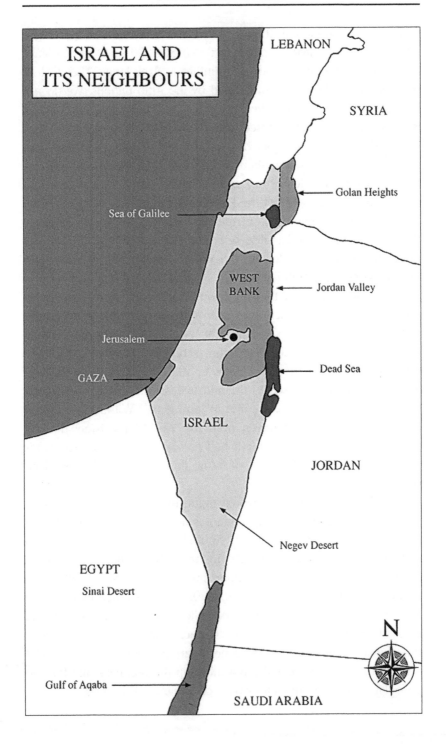

ISRAEL AND ITS NEIGHBOURS

LEBANON

SYRIA

Golan Heights

Sea of Galilee

WEST BANK

Jordan Valley

Jerusalem

Dead Sea

GAZA

ISRAEL

JORDAN

Negev Desert

EGYPT

Sinai Desert

N

Gulf of Aqaba

SAUDI ARABIA

They would argue that the world focuses on the Palestinian refugee problem, but is oblivious to the fact that 800,000 Jews had to leave or flee from long-established communities in Arab lands. They lost all their property which was confiscated by the Arab nations. We do not hear about these refugees, because most were assimilated into Israel, whereas the Arab states refused to settle the Palestinian refugees. They would also argue that Israel has refused re-entry for the Palestinian refugees and their descendants who now number several million, because Israel is a democracy and its Jewish nature would be voted out of existence as soon as the Palestinians were in a majority. Israel would argue that there is no reciprocity over the two sets of refugees: the Arab nations want Israel to settle the Palestinian refugees, but will not contemplate the settlement of Jewish people in a Palestinian state or in neighbouring Arab lands.

They would maintain that in 1967 neighbouring Arab states were openly preparing to attack and destroy Israel and that Israel fought a defensive war in which it came into possession of the West Bank, Gaza and the Golan Heights. It is on record that Israel asked Jordan, which had annexed the West Bank in 1950, to stay out of the war. This King Hussein refused to do, and instead his troops opened fire on Israel across the armistice line in Jerusalem.[15] Within days Jordan had been defeated and driven from the West Bank. Israel did not seek to occupy the West Bank. It had no plans or position papers for doing so.[16] Ironically, the seeds of future problems lay within this lack of preparedness.

Moving on in time, Israel would argue that it did eventually enter into negotiations for an independent Palestinian state which led to the Oslo Accords of 1993 and 1995, and which could have led to a conclusion at the Camp David talks in 2000. They would argue that the Palestinians missed their best opportunity for a negotiated settlement at this time. The Second Intifada followed and was much more deadly than the First Intifada thirteen years earlier. This time suicide bombers brought death and destruction into Israel proper. They would argue that the separation barrier was a necessary response to this – that it was the only way they could physically stop the bombers, and that no politician whether of the left or right could ignore this crisis.

What could Israel have done differently?

What Israel would have more difficulty in justifying is the way it has handled the occupation of the territories and in particular the West Bank. Once it had gained the West Bank and Gaza it had a responsibility for the way it managed them.

The very fact that it had no plans to occupy the West Bank in 1967 led to ineptitude in handling this unforeseen occupation. By this time Israel distrusted the idea of a Palestinian state because of the terrorist activities of the Palestine Liberation Organisation (PLO) and its declared intention to destroy Israel. Consequently, it refused to contemplate an autonomous Palestinian state or region. It seemed to envisage an indefinite occupation. The Palestinians became increasingly alienated and this led eventually to the First Intifada in 1987. This started as a popular movement of civil disobedience: strikes and refusal to pay taxes and took both the Israelis and the PLO leadership by surprise.[7] Benny Morris, a respected Israeli historian, says:

> *Israelis liked to believe, and tell the world, that they were running an "enlightened" or "benign" occupation qualitatively different from other military occupations the world has seen. The truth was radically different.* [17]

The handling of the occupation has not been the only issue. A subject which looms large in any discussion of the West bank is that of the Jewish settlements.[8] Settlers, whether to fulfil a religious or merely an expansionist dream, have sought to take back Judea and Samaria, the heartland of ancient Israel. These efforts were not held in check when they first started and have been allowed to happen ever since, so that there are now over 600,000 settlers in the West Bank and East Jerusalem. The government and military authorities allowed this to happen without thinking through the consequences. The settlements have caused controversy for several reasons, but the root cause is the fact that they have been built on land which is not part of the modern State of Israel. They are built on territory which was captured by Israel from Jordan in the Six-Day War of 1967.

Some Israelis argue that if a population of 20% Arabs can live in Israel proper then why should Jews not be allowed to live in the West Bank. There is indeed logic to this argument, but it comes with two caveats. The first concerns the status of the land. Israel argues that the West Bank is not occupied territory, but disputed territory. It argues that it has a right to settle in the West Bank because the Arabs refused to agree to partition in 1947. The land was never vested in a sovereign Palestinian state and so it is still part of the Mandate territory from the time of the League of Nations in 1922. The United Nations does not accept this reasoning. Israel's argument has two drawbacks. The first is that if the land is disputed then Israel needed to resolve the dispute before anticipating its outcome through settlement. The second is that by accepting the United Nation's partition plan in 1947 the Jews accepted a limit on the land they occupied as a nation, thereby recognising the reality of a Palestinian state in the rest of Palestine. It is true that the Arabs did not accept this proposal, but it is surely up to the United Nations, and not Israel, to recommend what happens to this land following the Arabs' rejection. The reality now is that the Palestinians do want their own state.

The second caveat is that the settlers needed to acquire the land legally. Sometimes this has not been the case. In the last ten years this problem has been severely compounded by the separation barrier. This was certainly started in a legitimate and desperate step to stop the suicide bombers and other terrorist activities.[18] It has now unfortunately come to represent the confiscation of Palestinian land and the cause of numerous indignities to the Palestinian people at large. The requisitioning of land in the West Bank and the means Israel uses to do it are well documented.[9]

Because the settlements have become so unpopular on the international stage, the Palestinians are unlikely to concede the argument that if Arabs can live in Israel then Jews should be able to live in the West Bank. Israel could have avoided this situation by reining in the movement in the aftermath of the Six-Day War. Israel as a nation is not united on the settlement policy. Many Jews are against it and recognise that many friends of Israel in the West have drawn the line at supporting Israel over the settlements. The nation has paid a heavy price in international support for allowing the settler movement to set the agenda.[19, 20]

God's perspective

The establishment of Israel and its relationship to its Palestinian neighbours has now evolved into a seemingly intractable problem. This seems an appropriate point to ask whether God has something to say about the restoration of the Jews and the establishment of the State of Israel. One may reasonably ask the question: if God wants the Jews back in the land then why have we arrived at such an unyielding situation in the Middle East? Why, for example, did he not allow the Jews to return to a virtually empty land and thus avoid a century of conflict?

The short answer is that we do not know. There are too many factors at work. However, there are two factors which suggest that God set the scene for a peaceful restoration of the Jews to their ancient land. The first is that there was plenty of land for both Jews and Palestinians to live in Palestine. Given that there were around 500,000 people in 1880 before the Jews began to return in significant numbers, and that today there are over 11 million people in Israel, the West Bank and Gaza, this fact seems indisputable (see Appendix 3, Population Statistics). The inhabited land does indeed have a high population density, but there is still plenty of land in the Negev Desert and the West Bank for enterprising Jews and Palestinians to bring into cultivation.

The second point is that the Palestinians could have had their own independent state, both in 1948 and again in more recent years. The Arabs were outraged at the United Nation's proposal to partition the land. However, partition of some sort was a realistic solution. It is an interesting fact that the President of the Palestinian Authority, Mahmoud Abbas, said in October 2011 that it was a mistake not to have accepted the United Nation's partition plan in 1947, a mistake he still hoped to rectify.[21]

What really matters, however, is what God has to say in the Bible. What he says there may provide a framework for understanding what is happening in the Middle East. To try and ascertain God's purposes is the aspiration of this book.

However, this is not as straightforward as it might seem. Given the complexity and divisiveness of what has happened in the Middle East, it is not surprising to find that there are different perceptions of the Bible narrative. This author believes that some of these perceptions are either selective or inaccurate – they do not look at the whole revelation concerning Israel. This happens on both sides of the argument. It is true of supporters of Israel who may be too confident about the meaning of end-time prophecy. They may also unwittingly overlook God's moral requirements in relation to the Israeli/Palestinian conflict. It is undoubtedly true of the opponents of Israel who throw into question the meaning of Old Testament text, and seldom make allowances for the unremitting hostility of the surrounding Arab and other nations.

Let us now take a comprehensive look at what God has to say on this vexed question of the restoration of the Jews and the re-establishment of the State of Israel. In doing this I am well aware that I am yet another person expressing his or her view of what the Bible has to say. This is why I use the expression: *comprehensive look at what God has to say.* I shall examine many scriptures in the attempt to establish the case I am making. I shall not duck the objections made by the opponents of this view, or skate over texts which might weaken this case. I am a scientist by training, so evidence is important to me. At the end of the book the reader must decide whether this evidence is convincing.

NOTES

1. Israel's heaviest losses were in the War of Independence (1948) when it lost 6,373 citizens from an initial population of 650,000 Jews (nearly 1%). (Source: Wikipedia, *List of wars involving Israel*; see also *Appendix 3*)

2. Calculated from data. (Source: Wikipedia, *List of countries and dependencies by area*). Arab countries included: Algeria, Saudi Arabia, Sudan, Libya, Egypt, Yemen, Morocco, Iraq, Oman, Syria, Tunisia, Jordan, United Arab Emirates, Kuwait, Qatar, Lebanon, Bahrain.

3. During the War of Independence (1948) and the years immediately after, approximately 800,000 Jews had to flee, or chose to leave, Arab lands where their families had often lived for centuries, in well-established Jewish communities. They were at risk and anti-Jewish riots led to killings in Aden, Egypt and Iraq. Nearly 600,000 were assimilated in Israel, while the rest settled in the United States and Western Europe. These refugees lost all their property in Arab lands. (Source: Many internet sites, e.g. Wikipedia, *Jewish exodus from Arab and Muslim countries*).

4. Both the President of Iran, Mahmoud Ahmadinejad, and the country's spiritual leader, Ayatollah Ali Khamenei, are openly on record as wanting the destruction of Israel. Source:

   Wikipedia, *Mahmoud Ahmadinejad and Israel*;

   Jerusalem Post 16 July 2012, quoting former Spanish Prime Minister José Aznar's conversation with Ayatollah Khamenei in 2000 <http://www.jpost. com/DiplomacyAndPolitics/Article.aspx?id=270185>

   A very good summary of President Ahmadinejad's many anti-Semitic and anti-Israel remarks can be found on the Anti-Defamation League website: <http://www.adl.org/main_International_Affairs/ahmadinejad_words.htm>

5. Israel's withdrawal from Gaza in 2005 did not bring peace. Since then several thousand rockets have been fired from Gaza into southern Israel, causing death, injury and psychological trauma to Israeli citizens. When from time to time Israel responds in a major way to these attacks, Western media frequently criticize Israel's response as disproportionate. In response to this, supporters of Israel ask: Would any Western government tolerate such attacks? Would we as its citizens expect them to tolerate such attacks?

   A Google search: Rocket attacks from Gaza into Israel brings up relevant websites.

   See: <http://www.idfblog.com/facts-figures/rocket-attacks-toward-israel/>

6. Israel has withdrawn from Gaza and from Area A of the West Bank, but access to Gaza and the West Bank is still restricted by Israel. See Glossary: *Oslo Accords* and *Palestinian Authority*.

7. See Glossary: *Intifada*.

8. The twenty-one Jewish settlements in Gaza were dismantled unilaterally by the Israeli Government led by Ariel Sharon in 2005.

9.   There are several organisations which monitor the development of settlements in the West Bank. Some of these draw their information from *B'Tselem*, a Jewish organisation within Israel, opposed to the settlement of the West Bank. This has been in existence since 1989 and its work is taken seriously by the Israeli authorities, even when they are unhappy with the content of its reports. (Source: Google search, *B'Tselem* then follow the links: *About B'Tselem* → *Land Expropriation and Settlements*; see also Benny Morris, *Righteous Victims* P.335). I recognise that this will make uncomfortable reading for supporters of Israel who are unfamiliar with what is happening in the West Bank. I recognise too that Israel disputes some of the legal arguments employed. However, I believe that we do have to face up to what is happening, and how this impacts the Palestinians.

10. See Glossary: *Green Line*.

11. See Glossary: *Oslo Accords* and *Palestinian Authority*.

12. This much quoted statement was made in a speech to the Knesset (Israel's Parliament) at the end of the Israeli-Lebanon conflict in 2006. (Source: The Globes – Israel's Business Arena 14 August 2006, main article. To find the article Google: *Olmert: We will continue to pursue Hizbullah's leaders*).

13. The United Nations voted for Resolution 181 which recommended the partition of Palestine into two independent states, one Jewish and one Arab, on 29 November 1947. With 72 countries voting in favour it received the required two-thirds majority. It was accepted by the provisional Jewish authority, the Jewish Agency and rejected by the leaders of the Arab nations including the Palestinian leaders. (Source: Wikipedia, *United Nations Partition Plan for Palestine*).

14. Following the defeat of the Ottoman Empire in World War I, Great Britain had been given the Mandate to govern Palestine by the League of Nations (predecessor to the United Nations) at the San Remo conference in 1920. Palestine had become increasingly volatile during the 1930s and the British Government found itself facing growing conflict, first with the Arab population and then after the Second World War with the Jews. It gave notice to the United Nations that it was relinquishing the Mandate and would withdraw completely by May 1948.

15. On the morning of 5 June 1967 Israel sent word to King Hussein through three separate channels saying Israel would honour the armistice agreement with his country, if Jordan were to stay out of the war, then commencing with Egypt and Syria. King Hussein ignored these warnings and his troops opened fire across the armistice line in Jerusalem. (Source: Benny Morris, *Righteous Victims* P.322-323).

16. Ibid. P.314.

17. Ibid. P.341.

18. The Israelis believe that the barrier eventually succeeded in stopping the bombings which ceased in 2006. The Palestinians dispute this and argue that

the cessation was a political decision. They argue that Hamas was about to enter elections and were persuaded that the attacks were counterproductive, both with their fellow Palestinians and internationally. Today with the barrier almost complete and Israel's massive security measures, it would be difficult to argue that it does not prevent suicide attacks. It does not prevent rocket attacks however, which still continue from Hamas controlled Gaza.

19. See Chapter 8 for a consideration of God's view of the land of Israel, and how we should approach this in today's world.

20. I recognise that the Settlements are a 'hot potato' with supporters and opponents of Israel debating the rights, legality and political wisdom of Jewish settlement in the West Bank. My own view is that supporters of Israel should be very cautious about anticipating God's purposes for the final boundaries of Israel. One of the unfortunate consequences of believing that Israel has a right to settle anywhere in its ancient territory of Judea and Samaria at the present time is to disparage the Palestinians. It disturbs me when I read articles by supporters of Israel which imply that the Palestinians do not really have a right to be in the land. Statements such as: "there never was a Palestinian state" or "the Palestinians thought of themselves as inhabitants of Southern Syria and only became known as Palestinians in the twentieth century" may be true, but they do not alter the fact that these people live in what has been known as Palestine since Roman times. Some Palestinians make exaggerated claims about how long they have lived there, but some families do not: they and their ancestors have lived in the land for centuries. Even if their ancestors arrived in the nineteenth and early twentieth centuries they still have rights: they will have bought property just as the Jews have done.

Their uprooting from what is now Israel was a grim consequence of the 1948 war, a war that was not of Israel's making. Many of these Palestinian refugees settled in the West Bank alongside Palestinians who were already there. It is understandable that Israel does not want to allow the return of descendants of these refugees, risking a majority Arab population which would overturn the Jewish nature of the state. However, it is reasonable to ask the question: Do supporters of Israel want to deny the Palestinians the right to live in the West Bank? If we argue for biblical reasons that the West Bank should now become part of Israel then where does that leave the Palestinians? This is a real, live 'facts on the ground' issue. It is not simply a theological issue. This is why I think we should exercise caution over anticipating God's purposes. After all he could have arranged for the land to be empty before the Jews returned, but he did not! In saying this I am not minimizing the provocations to Israel from its enemies who are not interested in peace, and the legitimate measures that Israel takes to protect its citizens.

21. Stated in an interview with Israeli Television Channel 2 and reported in Haaretz 28 October 2011. (Google search: *Haaretz – Abbas: Arab World was wrong to reject 1947 Partition Plan*).

2 *CONFLICTING THEOLOGIES*

||||||||||||||||||||||||||||| ||||||||||||||||||||||||||||||||||||||||||||||||||||||||||||||||||||||||||||||||||||||||||||||||||||

A friend who belongs to my prayer group for Israel and the Jewish people told me how she came to believe that such prayer was important.

Some years ago she was what she called "a baby Christian"; she had only been a believer in Jesus for a few months. One night she had a dream about a Father with two sons, one adopted and one biological. The biological son was in intensive care in a coma and every day the Father would visit his son. He just knew that one day this son would come out of his coma. When he tried to raise the subject with his much-loved adopted son, this son did not show any interest. This greatly upset the Father as he loved both very much and could not understand the adopted son's lack of interest for his brother. When my friend woke up she sensed that the Lord was showing her something close to Father God's heart and this eventually led her to read *Romans Chapter 11*. From then on she understood the importance of the Jewish people in God's eyes and that he wanted her to care about them too, she herself being part of the adopted son – a saved Gentile Christian.

For me this story captures exactly the reason why we should pray for Israel and the Jewish people. Several people I know who share this belief have felt such a calling, perhaps not so picturesque as this one, but nevertheless a distinct call. They sense that the Holy Spirit has alerted them, in the same way that other Christians sense the call to go on the mission field to a particular country, or to care for the poor in their home town.

This call is different from almost all the other calls by the Holy Spirit. If you tell the church that you have been called to the mission field in Africa for example, then everyone wishes you well and offers to pray that God will confirm the calling. If you tell people you have been called to pray for Israel and the Jewish people, it receives a mixed response. The evangelical Church, those who believe in a personal faith in Jesus Christ, is divided down the middle on this issue. There is a sharp divergence of views. It is not just about praying for Jews to receive salvation; few evangelicals would dispute the value of that. It is about supporting and praying for the nation of Israel and the Jewish people as a whole. It is about regarding the Jewish people as being in some way different from all other ethnic groups. It goes to the root of what Christians feel about the connection between the Old Testament and the New Testament in the Bible. In short, did God's interest in the Jewish people as a nation finish with the Old Testament or, in sharp contrast, does it persist until this day?

Christian Zionists and anti-Zionists

While many Christians are not concerned with this subject one way or the other, other Christians feel passionately about it. Those who think Israel is of continuing importance to God are often called **Christian Zionists** while those who think that God is now only concerned with the salvation of individual Jews, that he is no longer interested in Israel as a nation, are known as **Christian anti-Zionists**. The word **Zionist** means someone who supports the return of the Jews to the land of their ancestors and the re-birth of the nation of Israel. Clearly, there are many Zionists, mostly Jews, who are not Christians and who do not have a religious motive to support their view. As we shall see later, secular Jews, and a smaller number of religious Jews, have been returning to the land for over 100 years. (It is only fair to say that some Christian supporters of Israel do not like the label *Christian Zionist.* While supporting the return of the Jews to their ancient land they do not wish to be associated with the secular, political implications of the word *Zionist.*)

Anti-Zionist on the other hand means someone who is against the return of the Jews to the Holy Land, usually on the secular grounds that this has led to strife and turmoil in the Middle East. Christians, unless they believe that God has a continuing interest in the Jews as a nation, will tend to side with this secular view.

The return of the Jews to the Holy Land and the rebirth of the nation of Israel is one of the most written-about subjects in modern history. Israel and the Middle East are seldom out of the news. Supporters and opponents of Zionism battle it out in print and the subject is hotly contested. This battle of course spills out onto the streets of the Middle East, with rockets, bombs and bullets and unfortunately there is now real hatred between Zionists and anti-Zionists in this region. This book is primarily about the views of Christian Zionists and Christian anti-Zionists. While they are generally polite to each other, as behoves brothers and sisters in Christ, there is nevertheless a sharp polarisation of views. This is not just a good-natured difference of opinion. Representatives on both sides believe the other side holds views which are damaging to Christianity, to Israel and even to the world.

What is important to remember in this debate is God's purpose for the Jews at this time in history. *His purpose is paramount.* It is discerning this purpose that causes the dissension between the two sets of Christians.

It is important to engage with this issue because only one view is right. God either wants the Jews back in the land, or he does not. If we are wrong on the issue, but actively support our case, then we are working against God's purposes; Christian Zionists are furthering a cause without God's blessing and are doing so with the potential to cause trouble in the Middle East as Stephen Sizer alleges.[1] Alternatively, Christian anti-Zionists are discouraging the Church at a time when God wants the Church to stand with Israel and the Jewish people in prayerful support. Reaching a correct conclusion is therefore very important.

Approaches to end-time prophecy

So far we have contrasted Zionist with Anti-Zionist and Christian Zionist with Christian anti-Zionist. We need to be familiar with some other terms as well. The debate between the two schools of thought tends to be among evangelical Christians, that is to say, those who are "born again" or have a personal faith in Jesus Christ. In the broader Church, which does not necessarily subscribe to such a personal encounter with Jesus, people tend to view Israel only in a political context. Organisations such as the World Council of Churches take a political view of the Middle East and will support United Nations resolutions which condemn or criticise Israel. They will generally not see the Bible as predicting the future and they are concerned, as are many evangelicals, by the plight of the Palestinian people and in particular the Palestinian Christians.

This book is primarily concerned with the debate among evangelical Christians. My hope is to persuade both Christian anti-Zionists and the Church in general that the return of the Jewish people to Israel in the twentieth century is a fulfilment of prophecy and that we should therefore discern God's call to pray for the nation and the Jewish people. As we shall see in the final chapter, this can extend to praying for the Palestinian Church, the Palestinian Muslims and the wider Middle East.

The debate revolves around the fulfilment of what is called 'end-time prophecy' in the Bible. It is probably fair to say that all evangelicals believe in the second coming of Jesus Christ. They believe that at some point in history Jesus will return to earth. If one believes the Bible to be the Word of God it is really rather difficult to escape this conclusion. The New Testament has many references to Jesus' return. However, there are several very different views on how this will happen. The view taken revolves around what is known as the **Millennium**; this is a 1000-year reign before the final judgement of people's lives and before God winds up the present earth to create new heavens and a new earth. The four positions are: *Premillennialism, Postmillennialism, Amillennialism* and a more recent one, *Preterism*. These views are defined in the Glossary (*on the website*).

It is important to know that these alternative views exist, because only one of them, **Premillennialism**, attaches importance to the return of the Jews and the restoration of the nation of Israel. This view holds that Jesus will return at the end of the existing Church age to a world of increasing chaos and violence and that Israel will be back in the land. Having defeated Israel's foes, Jesus will usher in the 1000-year Millennial Kingdom.

Israel and the Jews have little or no place in the eschatological views of the postmillennial and amillennial believers or the preterists. They may believe that there will be a spiritual revival of the Jews based on *Romans Chapter 11*, but in not attaching biblical significance to the State of Israel they tend to see the state only in political and often negative terms.

Dispensationalism

A further term that needs defining is the term **Dispensational Christian Zionism.** Dispensationalism was established principally by John Nelson Darby, an English curate living in the early nineteenth century, and has been popularised in particular by American writers in the late twentieth century, people like Hal Lindsey, John Hagee and Tim LaHaye. The essence of this theology is that it is possible to divide the biblical history of the world into seven distinct periods, or dispensations. The two that are relevant to us are the last two: *the Church age* and *the Kingdom (millennial) age*, separated by the Second Advent or return of Christ. While there are clearly different phases in God's unfolding revelation to the human race, the Bible itself does not indicate any such division.

Problems with the Dispensational view

The dispensational view has not itself been consistent, but the principal problem is that it tends to speculate about the unfolding of future prophecy; subjects such as the *Return of Christ*, the *Rapture* and the *Great Tribulation*. While it is not wrong to think about the meaning of such prophecy, it is unwise to be too specific.

More traditional or **Classical Christian Zionism** on the other hand links the return of the Jews to the land of Israel with the *realised promises of God*, rather than with his future purposes. David Pawson[2] makes the important point that there is not a single explicit statement in the New Testament making the return of the Jews a sign of Jesus' return. The two may indeed be linked. There are indirect indications that Jerusalem will be in the hands of the Jews when Jesus returns (e.g. *Luke 13:35*), but we have no idea of the timescale. It is therefore unwise to build a theology which some Christian leaders then use as a 'blueprint' for action.

The distinction between classical and dispensational Christian Zionists is important if only because Christian anti-Zionists such as Stephen Sizer have a tendency to label all Christian Zionists as dispensational. This then suggests that they go along with the more melodramatic predictions of the popularisers of end-time prophecy who are all dispensationalists! This is not the case. One does not have to be a dispensationalist to believe that God has unfinished business with Israel.

Like David Pawson I would call myself a classical Christian Zionist because the main objective of this book is to demonstrate that the Old Testament predicts the return of the Jews to the land of Israel, something which has actually happened in modern times. I do believe that certain future events will be fulfilled literally. For example, I do believe that Zechariah's prediction that Jesus will return to the Mount of Olives (*Zechariah 14:4*) completes the promise in Acts (*Acts 1:11*) that Jesus will return in the same way as the apostles saw him ascend into heaven. However, I would not speculate about the timing of this event.

Christian anti-Zionism

We have now learnt something about Christian Zionism. What can we say about the theological position of the Christian anti-Zionists? There are really two streams to this: **Replacement Theology** and **Liberation Theology**. The first is a spiritual theology which has held sway in the Church for much of its existence, while the second is a much more recent theology which has now been adopted by Palestinian Christians. The underlying view of both theologies is that the return of the Jews to the land of Palestine in the last century, and the creation of the modern state of Israel, is contrary to biblical teaching.

Liberation theology came into being very much as a political movement, preaching a social gospel. It came into being in the second half of the twentieth century when Catholic priests in Latin America wanted to identify with the suffering of the poor and oppressed. Their mission came to be one of helping people to be free from colonial and economic oppression. Some became linked with political movements such as Marxism, while others argued that the way to resist such movements was for the Church to identify with the poor. This theology tends to be based on biblical passages which expound the justice and love of God and it may advocate political measures such as non-violent resistance. Palestinian liberation theology is a serious player in the Middle East since this theology has become international and interdenominational. The World Council of Churches (WCC) now supports the Palestinian Christians in their view of Israel as an oppressor nation. The WCC has 349 Church bodies and denominations as members and is highly influential in the Christian world.

Palestinian liberation theology (sometimes called *Christian Palestinianism*) is in part political and in part spiritual. Where it is political, as for example in the Kairos Palestine Document, I will leave the reader to make their own enquiries.[3] Where it challenges the literal understanding of the Old Testament prophecies then I will deal with it in Chapter 11, which follows the chapter on replacement theology.

Replacement theology is more purely theological. It has certainly had political consequences in history and its adherents may advocate political action today. However, it can stand alone as an understanding of the Bible in relation to Israel and the Old Testament covenants. Its supporters have a coherent theology to explain their point of view, but in my view it is one that is built on false premises.

For anti-Zionists to demonstrate that the return of the Jews and the creation of the modern state of Israel is not a fulfilment of Old Testament prophecy, they have to:

◊ express in some other way the many Old Testament prophecies that, taken literally, suggest the Jews will return to the Holy Land at some point in history.

◊ demonstrate that the covenant made with Abraham, Isaac and Jacob is not an everlasting covenant.

◊ confirm that God only has one chosen people at any point in history.

This theological position of the Christian anti-Zionist is variously known as:

◊   replacement theology
◊   fulfilment theology
◊   supersessionism, and more recently
◊   covenantalism

It puts much emphasis on New Testament revelation. It argues that all Old Testament prophecy should be seen through the lens of the New Testament. In the light of this revelation the Old Testament prophecies concerning Israel in the future are not to be taken literally. Instead they find their fulfilment in Jesus and/or the Church.

Replacement means that the Church has taken the place of Israel. *Fulfilment* means that the prophecies have been fulfilled in the person of Jesus Christ. *Supersessionism* comes from the word supersede and covers both replacement and fulfilment theology. **Covenantalism** means that the New Covenant inaugurated by Jesus has replaced the Old Covenant conveyed by Moses to the Jewish people at Mount Sinai. Adherents tend to see these two covenants as the two essential covenants, and very significantly they tend to treat the Mosaic and Abrahamic covenants as the 'Old Covenant'.[4] As we shall see in Chapter 7, the two need to be clearly differentiated.

Among traditional theologians the Christian anti-Zionist viewpoint holds sway. Popularisers of this position include Colin Chapman, Stephen Sizer and Gary Burge. Among the Palestinians they include Naim Ateek, Mitri Raheb and Yohanna Katanacho. These writers all have strong political views. Mention should also be made of the late William Hendriksen. There are others who are not political and not necessarily anti-Zionist. They include theologians such as David Holwerda and Wayne Grudem who nevertheless hold firmly to the view that the Old Testament promises have found their fulfilment in Jesus and/or the Church.

Christian Zionism received a tremendous boost with Israel's capture of the West Bank and East Jerusalem at the time of the Six-day War in 1967. Christians who had only taken a passing interest in Israel began to get excited at the thought that they might be witnessing the outworking of ancient prophecy before their very eyes. Bible teachers like Derek Prince had been teaching on the importance of Israel from its foundation in 1948, but it took the Six-Day War to bring about the spate of popular writings concerning the end times. As the occupation of the West Bank continued without resolution and Jewish people began to settle there, the early love affair with Israel manifested by so many secular left-wing people in the West began to wear off. Some Christians began to question Christian-Zionist assumptions about the fulfilment of prophecy in Israel. Colin Chapman was one of these early writers.

Covenantalists

From this point on I shall usually refer to the Christian anti-Zionists as **Covenantalists**. This is Stephen Sizer's term[5] and it is more concise than *Replacement Theologians* or *Fulfilment Theologians*. We shall examine replacement theology and its origin in Church history in Chapter 10 and see that it did cause terrible suffering to the Jews. However, I wish to emphasise that I do not ascribe the Church's anti-Semitism throughout much of its history to Christian writers today, who genuinely subscribe to some form of replacement theology in the belief that it is theologically correct.

However, I need to make very clear at this point that I am responding to the theological views of these covenantalist writers. I am not engaging with their politics. Some of these evangelical writers have adopted political stances towards the State of Israel which are highly antagonistic and which I believe distort their understanding of Scripture. Furthermore, it has led some western supporters of the Palestinians, notably the Anglican vicar, Rev Stephen Sizer, to reach out to some strange companions in the Middle East. It saddens me that Sizer is now so negative towards Israel and the supporters of Israel. This has led to him attending conferences and associating with Muslim clerics and others who are both anti-Semitic and who advocate violence towards Israel and its Jewish citizens. He argues that while he is anti-Zionist, he is not anti-Semitic. He might demonstrate this more convincingly by choosing not to identify with people who have publicly shown their antipathy for Jews.[6]

End-time prophecy

Given the charge by some anti-Zionists that Christian Zionists are dispensationalists, I need to express a personal point of view. When it comes to end-time prophecy I cannot agree with Christian Zionist leaders such as John Hagee when they call for political and military action in relation to Israel. At the launch of his organisation, Christians United for Israel, in Washington in July 2006, he is reported to have said:

> The United States must join Israel in a pre-emptive military strike against Iran to fulfil God's plan for both Israel and the West... a biblically prophesied end-time confrontation with Iran, which will lead to the Rapture, Tribulation... and Second Coming of Christ.[7]

Hagee's concerns about Iran's nuclear threat to Israel are certainly valid, but as Christians we are called to pray for solutions, not to implement them. It is up to God how he chooses to use governments and secular bodies to achieve his objectives.

End-time prophecies are also problematical in another way. From the 1970's onwards the evangelical Christian world was inundated with books about the end-times by popular writers such as Hal Lindsey. There are two risks attached to such writing: one is an unhealthy desire to hasten the return of the Lord. For premillennialists this follows a period of unparalleled trouble on earth, where Israel is right at the centre of this trouble. One can rightly surmise that Jewish people who know about this are not very keen on such predictions and some even distrust Christian motives for supporting Israel and the Jewish people.

The other risk is that when specific prophecies do not materialise, it discredits the legitimate place of prophecy in understanding the Bible. I am not comfortable with the popularisation of prophecy that has not happened. This is especially popular in the United States. I think by now evangelical Christians should be wise to the fact that God plays things close to his chest and attempts to make specific prophecies such as the end-time role of the European Union or the Catholic Church, or even likely candidates for the antichrist, usually come to nought and 'the prophets' have to revise their views.

However, when we look back on certain events in the last century to do with Israel, I think we are on much safer ground in seeing such events as a fulfilment of prophecy.

Objectives of this book

So what do I believe and what do I hope to demonstrate in this book? I shall attempt to show that the current return of the Jews to the Holy Land is a fulfilment of Old Testament biblical prophecy and furthermore that in doing this God is honouring his Covenant to Abraham, Isaac and Jacob. I shall demonstrate that there is no conflict between Israel as a nation and the Church. The New Covenant inaugurated by Jesus is a culmination of the Mosaic Covenant and as such it completes and therefore takes the place of the Law, but it in no way supersedes the Abrahamic Covenant. Individually, people find salvation through the sacrificial death and resurrection of Jesus, whether they be Jews or Gentiles. They enter the spiritual kingdom of God and constitute his new creation, the Church.

However, there are sound scriptural reasons for arguing that the Jewish people and nation have not been discarded, forgotten about or somehow absorbed into the rest of humanity. There are good reasons for arguing that God has unfinished business with the Jews and that he will bring them to a place where as a people they will recognise Jesus, himself a Jew, as their Messiah. God will do this in part because they rejected his Son and failed to see who he was on his First Advent and in part because he has a special relationship with Israel. In the book of Isaiah (*Isaiah 54:5-6*) he talks of Israel as his wife. Marriage is a covenant relationship. Although Israel has disappointed God in the past I believe he is determined to demonstrate that this marriage will work! The phrase: *God has unfinished business with the Jews as a people* really represents the theme of this book.

While recognising that God has dealings with groups of people, such as nations, I believe profoundly that individual Jews must come to a saving faith in Jesus Christ, just like the Gentiles. I emphasise this throughout the book and cannot agree with that small number of Christian Zionists who believe that God saves the Jews on the basis of being Jewish and not through the atoning death of Jesus on the Cross. (See Glossary: *Dual-Covenant Theology*.)

If I succeed in persuading the reader that these events are in accordance with Scripture, then I also hope to persuade them of the importance of prayer for Israel and the Jewish people. This is covered in the last chapter.

NOTES

1. Stephen Sizer, *Zion's Christian Soldiers* P.19.

2. David Pawson, *Defending Christian Zionism* P.33.

3. World Council of Churches website: <http://www.oikumene.org/> and search for the Kairos Palestine Document. Alternatively see: Yohanna Katanacho, *The Land of Christ – A Palestinian Cry* P.143.

4. See Stephen Sizer, *Zion's Christian Soldiers* P.63 where he says: *"The promises made to Abraham were, however, conditional."* This is not so; the conditions were attached to the Mosaic Covenant, not the Abrahamic Covenant. This distinction between the two covenants is emphasised in the New Testament Book, *Hebrews*, where the author talks about the permanence of the Abrahamic Covenant in *Chapter 6* and the temporal nature of the Mosaic Covenant in *Chapter 8*.

5. Ibid. P.12-13.

6. Stephen Sizer is quite open about his association and photographic opportunities with Muslim opponents of Israel. These include the Grand Mufti or Muslim spiritual leader of Jerusalem Sheikh Muhammud Hussein, Zahra Mostafavi of Iran and Sheikh Raed Salah, a leader of the Muslim Movement in Israel. Such association does not in itself make Sizer anti-Semitic, but it seems very unwise in such a polarized part of the world. There does not appear to be any corresponding association with Israeli political and religious leaders which might redress this bias.

   These are some of the many websites which refer to his or their views:

   Stephen Sizer: <http://www.stephensizer.com> Click on Photos and Blog.

   Palestine Media Watch: <http://www.palwatch.org/> See video: *PA Mufti calls for killing of Jews quoting Islamic Hadith* (9th January 2012). The video introduces the Grand Mufti with the words of the Moderator at a meeting of the Palestinian political party Fatah: *"Our war with the descendants of the apes and pigs (i.e. the Jews) is a war of religion and faith. Long Live Fatah! [I invite you] our honourable Sheikh"*.

   New York Sun: Mostafavi's support for suicide bombers is reported in an article on 16 August 2006.

   <http://www.nysun.com/foreign/islamic-leaders-urge-children-to-be-bombers/38023/>

   Huffington Post /Alan Johnson, *We still should not invite Raed Salah to Tea* (14th April 2012) <http://www.huffingtonpost.co.uk/alan-johnson/>

7. See website: NEWSMAX.COM, *Pastor John Hagee's D.C. Meeting Worries Jews* (17 May 2007) <http://archive.newsmax.com/archives/articles/2007/5/16/211015.shtml>

3 HAS GOD BEEN ASLEEP FOR THE LAST 130 YEARS?

This cryptic chapter title highlights a serious objection to Covenantalism. Since 1882 the Jewish people have been returning or making *aliyah* to the Holy Land and in 1948 the nation of Israel was reborn under the auspices of the United Nations. This return has happened either with God's full sanction and in fulfilment of his purposes for the Jewish people at this time in history or the Jews have slipped back "under his nose" so to speak, and are occupying the former land without his permission. It is difficult to envisage an alternative explanation.

God's sovereign and discretionary will

I suggest that most evangelical Christians would subscribe to the view that God exercises his will in one of two ways. There is God's sovereign will and his discretionary (or permissive) will. His sovereign will concerns his foreordained purposes for the human race in history and these he will not change. They are bound to happen. His discretionary will concerns the way he allows his plans to unfold and here he permits an interaction with the way human beings behave. He will reach his goal, but not necessarily by his preferred route. If he did not do this he would exclude a defining feature of human beings, their free will.

An example of his sovereign will is the covenant he made with Abraham to create a great nation through the line of Isaac and Jacob. This became the nation of Israel. An example of his discretionary will happens at the time of the golden calf incident (*Exodus Chapter 32*). Moses is on Mount Sinai for forty days in the presence of God and the

Israelites persuade Aaron to make an idolatrous golden calf. In his fury God purposes to destroy the Israelites leaving only Moses and his family through whom he says he will make a great nation. Moses, in a fine example of intercessory prayer, persuades God to change his mind and stick to his original plan. The interesting thing about this incident is that God could still have fulfilled his sovereign promise to Abraham, but in a rather different way from that which he originally intended.

We have only to follow the subsequent history of Israel in the Old Testament to see God's sovereign and discretionary will in operation. He allows human will much leeway and pleads with the Israelites to be obedient and not to go after idols (his discretionary will), but when they finally refuse to repent he sends them into exile. His purposes will not be thwarted.

The only way we can ascertain his sovereign will is to go to Scripture where we can read his covenants, his promises and his prophecies. We need to bear this in mind when we try to sort out the rift that has arisen between the Christian Zionists and the Christian anti-Zionists: that is between those who support Israel and the return of the Jewish people to the land, and those who do not or have grave doubts about it.

An accident of history?

Meanwhile let us return to the question of God's sovereign and discretionary will. The question for the Covenantalists is this: Is the return of the Jews and the re-establishment of the nation of Israel an accident of history? Has God let it happen under his discretionary will but would much rather it had not happened, or is it his sovereign will for the Jewish people? I believe that an extensive examination of the Old Testament prophecies concerning Israel will demonstrate that it is his sovereign will. If it is not, then it must be very painful for him. The Middle East is hardly ever out of the news. Israel and its relationship with its Arab neighbours occupies an enormous amount of news coverage. It distracts thousands of Christians, but most serious of all, Israel's presence in the Middle East threatens to blow up into a worldwide nuclear conflagration. This could destroy thousands, perhaps millions of both Christians and unbelievers. Now that would seriously affect God's plan of salvation and must surely impact his sovereign will!

The Covenantalist may object that the threat of nuclear war is still there but if Israel's re-establishment in the Middle East is God's sovereign will, then we can have confidence that major developments will also be under his control.

The return of the Jews

Today we are confronted with the return of several million Jews to the land of Palestine and the existence of the State of Israel. Two hundred years ago leading British Christians were reading the scriptures and beginning to believe that God intended to restore the Jewish people to their homeland, 1700 years after their final expulsion from Jerusalem and the land at the end of the first century (AD 135). This included statesmen like Lord Shaftesbury, Lord Palmerston and William Wilberforce, and ministers such as the Reverend Murray McCheyne and Charles Spurgeon. In fact some Puritan Christians as early as Cromwell's time in the 1650s were beginning to think this way.

At that time sceptics could be forgiven for thinking that these people were wrong, that it was a mere pipedream. The Ottoman Empire had let the land of Palestine become a backwater. They had instituted a bizarre tax on trees which meant the land became deforested in order to avoid the tax. The land had ceased to thrive and remained under-populated for centuries. This is attested by people who visited the land in the nineteenth and early twentieth centuries. They included prominent European visitors to the land, people such as the British consul to Jerusalem, James Finn, in the 1850s and the American writer Mark Twain in 1867.[1] It was also seen by ordinary people like the soldiers under General Allenby when he took Jerusalem from the Ottomans in 1917.[2] Overall, Palestine was not a thriving agricultural land. It had areas of productive Arab farming with fertile soil supporting cereals and fruit trees but much of the land was stony and uncultivated, or in low lying areas, swampy and in need of drainage.[3]

There were also some Jewish rabbis in the nineteenth century who expressed the view that the Jews needed to be back in their ancient land in order to meet their Messiah, though they were very much in a minority among orthodox Jews. This included Rabbi Judah Alkalai of Serbia, Rabbi Zvi Kalischer of Poland and the late Rabbi Abraham Kook of Latvia who emigrated to Palestine in 1904. It is true that a trickle of Jews had returned to the land over the centuries to escape persecution, usually and regrettably from Christian countries. However by the nineteenth century the number of Jews in the Holy Land had remained small, at about 24,000 in 1880. The population of indigenous Arabs, while considerably larger than the Jews at 470,000, was also small in relation to the size of the land.

The first aliyah

Despite the regular persecution of Jews and pogroms across Europe and Russia, there had never been large-scale migration to escape this persecution by returning to Palestine. This did not begin to happen until 1882 with the First Aliyah or emigration to their ancient homeland. These were predominantly secular Jews fleeing from pogroms in Russia. Many left Russia in the 1880s and 1890s but only a small portion (2% annually) went to Palestine. Most went to the USA or Britain. Nevertheless this still meant that 25,000 Jews reached Palestine by the end of the First Aliyah (1903). In 1904 a second wave of immigration began which lasted ten years until the outbreak of the First World War This was known as the Second Aliyah and was to escape the more widespread pogroms in Russia, Poland and other parts of Eastern Europe. This time the number was larger. This was still a minority of Jews leaving these areas of persecution. According to one estimate the Jewish population in Palestine in 1914 was now 85,000. These two aliyahs were the start of a much larger return of Jews in the twentieth century (see Appendix 3).

The question inevitably arises as to why this did not happen earlier in history. There were no shortages of opportunity. In the Middle Ages Jews were sometimes expelled en masse from a country. Why did the Jews, who were expelled from Britain in 1290 by Edward I, not return to the Holy Land? In 1492 around 90,000 Jews who refused conversion to Christianity were expelled from Spain. Some of these returned to the Holy Land where they revitalised Jewish life in the Galilee, but the great majority went elsewhere in Europe, North Africa and the Ottoman Empire. In the seventeenth century Russian Cossacks joined with Polish peasants in attacking the Jews and over 100,000 were killed. Many fled to Holland, Germany and the Balkans. Like their predecessors they too did not flee to the Holy Land.[4]

In the nineteenth century the initial immigrants were primarily secular Jews. They sought a place of refuge rather than a spiritual home. They purchased land, often from absentee landlords, and they settled as farmers, draining swamps and establishing the Jewish co-operative villages known as kibbutzim. Life was hard for these early settlers and many died from malaria.

If God was calling them back to the land, then for the most part these early settlers did not know it, and yet they came. What started as a small emigration in the 1880s snowballed in the twentieth century to a much larger immigration, especially once the State of Israel had been created. This followed the Holocaust of the Second World War when six million Jews were executed, or died in Nazi concentration camps. In the immediate aftermath of this war the nations were sympathetic to the establishment of a homeland for the Jews. The newly established United Nations voted for the establishment of a Jewish state and an Arab state in 1947.

Next year in Jerusalem?

Despite the well-known Jewish greeting at the end of Passover: "Next year in Jerusalem!" this return did not transpire over the centuries. Something seemed to hold the Jews back year after year and then something seemed to release them to return. I think most evangelical Christians would accept that God often prefers to work behind the scenes. I have no difficulty in believing that at a certain point in history he released the Jews to return to the land. The Bible puts it rather picturesquely: *"I will whistle for them and gather them in," Zechariah 10:8* and *Isaiah 5:26.* Furthermore, parts of the Protestant Church, especially in Britain, felt called to pray and thus facilitate this process. As you will see later in the book, I strongly believe that in this Church era God uses the Church to intercede on behalf of the things he wishes to bring about. He does not have to do it this way, but he seems to want to involve his people in doing his work.

I remember talking to an elderly Jewish couple in Jerusalem who had lived in England and then emigrated to Israel twenty-five years ago. When I asked them why they had come they said: *"It just seemed the right thing to do"*. I have heard of other Jews who expressed similar views. They do not attribute it to the call of God, but they seem to have a sense that they are being drawn to the land. Those Christians who are antagonistic to the return of the Jews seem to forget that many in the western nations do not want to uproot and leave a comfortable existence behind. They are not exactly emigrating to a peaceful part of the world! Many Jews are unhappy and disorientated when they arrive in Israel – for a start they have to learn a completely new language. Some even return home to the country they came from. I maintain that something (the Holy Spirit) is drawing them back and sometimes against their better judgement! In Chapter 5 we will examine the prophecies which substantiate this view.

The God of history

Let us not forget that God is the God of history. He declares many times that he is behind history. Let us look at two of the scriptures

> God makes nations great, and he destroys them; he enlarges nations and disperses them.
>
> (Job 12:23; NIV)

> And he made from one man every nation of mankind to live on all the face of the earth, having determined allotted periods and the boundaries of their dwelling place, that they should seek God, in the hope that they might feel their way towards him and find him.
>
> (Acts 17:26-27)

Do we seriously think that a God who is in charge of history has allowed the nation of Israel to arise without his approval – a nation so significant in biblical history? I think not. God does not declare his impotence in the face of empires and nations. He declares his power!

Stephen Sizer agrees with this point when he quotes from Isaiah (*Isaiah 63:3-6*) which describes God's wrath concerning the nations and then says:

> If this is the context for Jesus' words, then we learn from Isaiah that even the most powerful of human tyrants and empires are subject to God's sovereign will, and in some mysterious way fulfil his purposes and judgements.[5]

Is Sizer arguing that despite empires being subject to God's sovereign will, a nation like Israel is somehow outside of it? Is he saying that Israel has come into being only through God's discretionary will?

Has God been asleep?

I believe the continued existence of Israel demonstrates the ongoing significance of the Jewish people. Its existence, its revival as a nation in the twentieth century, is powerful evidence that the Jews as a nation are still part of God's plan. After all, the Covenantalists would have us believe that Israel is now just another nation among many others. I hope this chapter demonstrates that Israel's restoration is unlikely to be outside of God's sovereign will. I make this observation even before we start to examine the Old Testament prophecies which predict it!

No, God has not been asleep. The Psalmist declares:

> *He who keeps you will not slumber. Behold, he who keeps Israel will neither slumber nor sleep.*
>
> (*Psalm 121:3-4*)

From modern times to Israel's early history

This whole debate is generated by the fact that Israel was exiled by God from the Promised Land several centuries before the birth of Christ and then again in the first century AD. These exiles were associated with promises of a return to the land, part of which was fulfilled in the return from Babylon and part of which remains to be fulfilled. The crux of the debate centres on what is understood by these further promises. In the next two chapters we shall take a look at the captivity and exile of Israel and then examine Scriptures which relate to the return from exile. As the reader follows the history and reads the many Scriptures, I ask him or her to assess whether they think the scriptures should be taken literally. We will come back to this point in Chapter 6 when we examine ways in which the Bible can be read.

NOTES

1. James Finn – Google search: Ruth Kark, *Changing patterns of land ownership in nineteenth-century Palestine: The European Influence* P.359 (Journal of Historical Geography, 10, 4, 1984).

    Mark Twain, *The Innocents Abroad* 1869 (Quoted in Wikipedia, *Demographics of Palestine*, Section: Traveller's impressions of 19th Century Palestine).

2. Personal communication from a friend whose father was a soldier in General Allenby's army.

3. This image of nineteenth century Palestine, and Mark Twain's account in particular, are disputed by Palestinian writers. Wikipedia, *Demographics of Palestine*, gives a variety of travellers' views and Mark Twain himself was complimentary about Arab agriculture when he came across it. One Jewish writer, Ahad Ha'am, a forthright critic of the early Zionist settlers, wrote in 1891:

    > It is very difficult to find in the land cultivated fields that are not used for planting. Only those sand fields or stone mountains that would require the investment of hard labour and great expense to make them good for planting, remain uncultivated.

    He might have added swampland! However this inhospitable land, of which there was much, was exactly the land on which so many kibbutz villages were established.

    What seems to me indisputable is that the land was under-populated and that the Ottomans made no effort to encourage agriculture – in fact, exactly the opposite, as they taxed every farm animal and every fruit tree. There is evidence that villages became deserted as a result of this discouragement of agriculture and that the nomadic Bedouin took the place of the settled Fellaheen (Arab peasant farmers) in the Jordan Valley. (See H B Tristram 1856, quoted in the Wikipedia article above).

    The fact that today's population is over twenty times larger than it was in 1880 (11 million versus 500,000) supports this argument. The inhospitable nature of much of the terrain is testified by the work of removing stones and rocks and draining swamps in the newly-formed kibbutz villages (See Yehuda Avner, *The Prime Ministers* P.75-76). One of the first things the early Jewish settlers did was to start to repopulate the land with trees, natural forest as well as fruit trees. A look at Israel from the air using *Google Earth* will illustrate the amazing transformation wrought by Israeli agriculture in the north and middle sections of the country.

4. Max Dimont, *Jews, God and History* P.228, 230, 245-246; Martin Gilbert, *The Routledge Atlas of Jewish History* P.56

5. Stephen Sizer, *Zion's Christian Soldiers* P.109

4 *CAPTIVITY AND EXILE: THE FIRST RETURN FROM EXILE*

Before we look at the prophecies concerning the return of the Jews to the land of Israel, we need to review some history and to define some significant events.

A brief history

The united nation of **Israel** reached the height of its powers under King David and his son, King Solomon, around 1000 BC. David was the warrior king of the tribe of Judah. He subdued the surrounding nations, such as the Philistines, while Solomon reaped the benefits and ruled a nation which displayed God's glory through its Temple and the power and riches of the nation. (*For a map of this kingdom see Chapter 8.*) However, due to Solomon's apostasy later in life – he married many foreign women and was seduced into worshipping their foreign gods – God became disappointed and angry with him and he divided his kingdom after Solomon's death. He allowed his descendants to rule in the smaller kingdom only (*1 Kings 11:1-13*). God did not do this for Solomon's sake, but for the sake of David his father and the covenant he had made with him (*2 Samuel 7:1-17*).

Judah became the southern kingdom with Solomon's descendants as kings in the capital Jerusalem. It also included the smaller tribe of Benjamin and the priests and Levites who served in the Temple. **Israel** on the other hand included the remaining ten tribes, initially under a king called Jeroboam, and based around the capital of Samaria.

This distinction between Judah and Israel becomes a major theme for the remainder of the Old Testament. This is the era of the great prophets. They were sent by God to one or other nation and sometimes to both nations. They also gave prophecies concerning the nations which surrounded Judah and Israel.

Both Judah and Israel displeased God, and the prophets time and again called the kings and the people of both nations to turn back to their God. Eventually God acted according to his warnings which had first been given by Moses, and repeated many times by the prophets, that he would exile the people from the land which he had given to them as an inheritance. All the kings of Israel did evil in God's sight which is why the ten tribes went into exile before Judah. Some of the kings of Judah were good in God's sight, for example Jehoshaphat, Hezekiah and Josiah. However, the evil of its bad kings, like Manasseh, ultimately constrained the Lord to send them into exile as well (*see the accompanying map of the two kingdoms*).

Going back in history, the Jews first became a nation at the time of the Exodus from Egypt (circa 1400 BC), and their settlement in the land of Canaan. This happened under the leadership first of Moses and then of Joshua. Although the patriarchs Abraham, Isaac and Jacob had dwelt in the land with their families, this did not count as occupancy of the land by a nation. Jacob and his descendants were at most a large family or clan, when seventy of them went down into Egypt to be reunited with Jacob's son, Joseph. Furthermore, they went down voluntarily. This is a very important point. The Exodus, which looms large in Jewish history, led to the establishment of the nation of Israel under its twelve tribes (plus the priesthood) in the land of Canaan.

This Exodus is sometimes described by Covenantalists as a return to the land and bracketed with the later return from the exile in Babylon. This enables them to call the return from Babylon a second return and then argue, as Stephen Sizer does, that the Bible does not speak of a third Jewish return.[1] While technically it is a return in the sense that Jacob's descendants came back, it is most definitely not a return from exile, nor is it the return of a nation. The nation commenced at the time of the Exodus when God inaugurated the Mosaic Covenant and gave the Israelites statutes and laws for operating as a nation. The significance of this point will become apparent when we consider the two exiles and the two returns from exile.

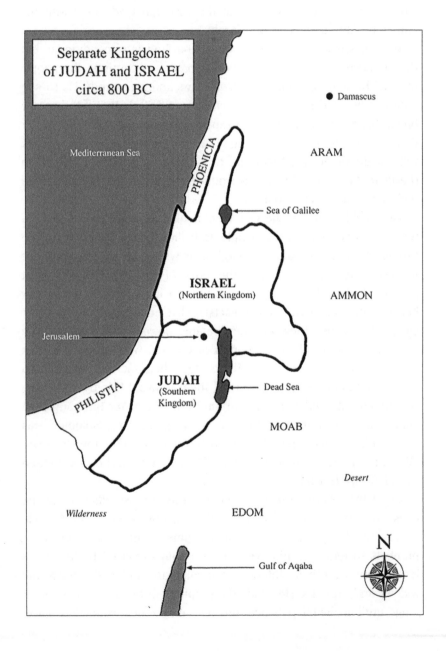

The exiles came many centuries later. They happened in response to the people's continued disobedience to God's laws and statutes which were given to Moses on Mount Sinai (*Deuteronomy 29:1*) at the time of the founding of the nation. We will examine the right to live in the land of Canaan when we look at the covenant God made with the patriarchs Abraham, Isaac and Jacob.

We will see that the possession of the land is unconditional, but that its occupation is not. For its occupation to continue the people of Israel have to be obedient to God's laws and commands. He says in both *Leviticus 26:32-33* and *Deuteronomy 28:63-64* that if the people break this covenant then he will expel them from the land and scatter them among the nations. It is significant however that he also says he will not utterly destroy them and thus break his covenant with them (*Leviticus 26:44-45*). To do this would be to break the covenant with their forefathers, the patriarchs.

We quickly learn in the Old Testament that Israel proves to be a rebellious and stiff-necked people. Rebellion begins en route to the Promised Land, and although God deals with it harshly, it continues to resurface, especially after the time of Joshua. The sin most grievous to God is idolatry, the worship of idols. This is not simply because they are inanimate objects and a huge insult to Almighty God, but because they represent satanic powers and demons, (see *1 Corinthians 10:20*). The peoples of Canaan were steeped in this kind of idolatrous worship with its degrading sacrifice of children and sexual immorality. God warned them to avoid this by destroying the inhabitants and not intermarrying with them. Yet time and time again they succumbed to this. Even the great King Solomon was seduced into worshipping false gods through his many foreign wives. His initial sin was to marry outside of Israel, since God had forbidden this (*1 Kings 11:1-2*).

Given the severity with which God warned the Israelites about the consequences of sin, it is amazing that he was so long-suffering. He pleads with his people all through the time of the major and minor prophets to return to him. He was especially exercised by the sin of idolatry, but also their attitude to the vulnerable in Jewish society, the widows and orphans. He sends the prophets through a succession of kings, until finally his patience runs out and the first exile takes place.

An overview of the exiles

For the Christian who is new to the history of Israel it is important to understand that there were two exiles. The first took place in the first millennium BC several centuries before the time of Christ. This applied to both the kingdom of Israel and the kingdom of Judah, but at different times. The first return from exile was a limited return and applied predominantly to the people of Judah who were in exile in Babylon. Most of the people from Israel and many of the people from Judah remained in exile at this time, founding communities in the Middle East and along the North African coast which survived until the middle of the twentieth century AD.

The second exile occurred in the century after the time of Christ. This was an exile of the descendants of those who had returned from the captivity in Babylon. This exile left only a tiny remnant of Jews living in the land for the next 1800 years, until modern times.

Christian Zionists consider the modern day return of the Jews to be a second return from exile, one that was predicted by the prophets over 2500 years ago. Christian anti-Zionists dispute that these prophecies apply to the modern day return of the Jews. They argue either that all the prophecies can be explained in the limited return from the Babylonian captivity or more usually that these prophecies are not to be taken literally, that they have a different meaning by the time we reach the New Testament. As already indicated one of the objectives of this book is to demonstrate that these prophecies do apply to a second return from exile. This second return can only be the modern day return of the Jews, since there has been no other return to follow the limited return from Babylon.

The first exile

The First Exile took place in two phases. To begin with the northern state of Israel (the ten tribes) were taken captive. This took place over a number of years, but is usually denoted by the date 721 BC when its principal town of Samaria was captured by the Assyrians.

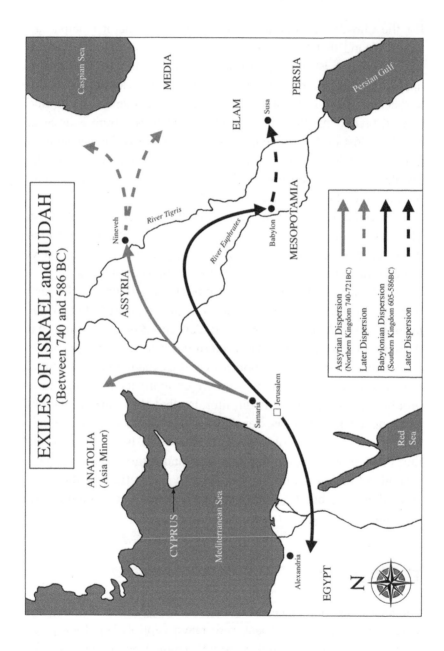

EXILES OF ISRAEL and JUDAH
(Between 740 and 586 BC)

The exiles were dispersed and located in all parts of the Assyrian empire. This was later followed by the exile of Judah which was completed in 586 BC with the destruction of Jerusalem and the Temple. The tribes of Judah and Benjamin along with the priests and Levites were taken captive to Babylon by King Nebuchadnezzar in three stages, beginning in 605 BC. Some were also taken to Egypt. It is significant for future history that the northern tribes were dispersed, while the southern tribes were mostly located in and around Babylon (*see the accompanying map of the exiles of Israel and Judah*).

We have a clear record of their history in Babylon, for example in the books of Daniel and Ezekiel, and we have some information from secular sources. We also have a clear record of the return of some of the exiles in the book of Ezra, at the end of the seventy-year period predicted by Jeremiah (*Jeremiah 25:8-14*). The Jews were given permission by Cyrus, king of the Medo-Persian Empire, to return to Jerusalem to rebuild the Temple under Zerubbabel. The book of Ezra (*Ezra Chapter 2*) suggests that about 50,000 people made this return journey. Of these about 30,000 belonged to the tribes of Judah, Benjamin and Levi. Some of the people from the ten tribes were also located in and around Babylon and it has been inferred that about 12,000 of these likewise made the journey.[2] The remainder and their families were servants. Much smaller numbers returned first with Ezra and then with Nehemiah 70-80 years later to rebuild the walls of Jerusalem. Thus the return from the first exile is well documented and it was a limited return. (*See Appendix 4 for a more detailed account of the exile and captivity, and reference to secular sources.*)

The second exile

The Second Exile took place after the death and resurrection of Jesus, first in AD 70 when the Roman general Titus laid siege to and conquered Jerusalem, and then finally in AD 135 when the Romans tried to erase all evidence of the Jews and renamed the land Palestine. Those not killed were taken captive to Rome and then out into the Empire to add to the descendants of those already dispersed following the first exile several hundred years earlier. We know from the book of Acts that the apostle Paul was able to visit Jewish communities all over the Roman Empire. He went first to the synagogue before he preached to the Gentiles. This was before the second exile under the Romans. This is testimony to the fact that many Jews had not returned with the exiles from Babylon under the leadership of Zerubbabel, Ezra and finally Nehemiah. Instead they had settled to form communities while also retaining their distinct identity as Jews. The descendants of all these dispersed Jews are known as the *Diaspora* and, apart from a very small remnant, have not lived in the land for between 1800 and 2500 years.[3] (*See Appendix 5 for a more detailed discussion of the second exile.*)

It seems likely that the Second Exile was God's response to the nation's rejection of Jesus at his First Advent. The leaders and much of the nation rejected their Messiah. There is a move among some Christian Zionists today to exonerate the Jews from Jesus' rejection at the time of Calvary. In my view this is mistaken and an inappropriate way to atone for the anti-Semitism of the Church through much of its history.

How else are we to explain the severity of the second exile in AD 70 when the Temple and Jerusalem were razed to the ground? This is not to say that the ordinary Jewish people wanted Jesus to die. The High Priest and other leaders clearly did, as they plotted to kill him from early in his ministry. However, it is true to say that the nation to whom he came as their Messiah did not receive his teaching. Many followed him at first and then fell away when the teaching became harder to receive (*John 6:66-69*).

We need to put this in perspective. Ultimately we are all responsible for the death of Jesus, Gentile and Jew alike, because it was our sin which caused him to go to the Cross and die on our behalf. Amazingly, this was foreordained by God (*Acts 2:23*) because he was determined to reconnect with the human race, while at the same time upholding his righteous judgement of sin. In scapegoating the Jews during its appalling history of anti-Semitism, the Church failed to remember this simple fact.

The point of contention

The debate between the Christian Zionists and the anti-Zionists hinges on the exile, and return from exile, of the Jewish people. There is general agreement about the two exiles and the return from the first exile because these are past events and evangelical Christians agree on the historical reliability of the Bible. The dispute is about whether the Bible predicts a further return from the Diaspora that existed in the first century AD after the final exile under the Romans. To establish the Christian Zionists' position, we need to demonstrate that the Old Testament predicts two returns from exile and that these two returns are differentiated sufficiently to demonstrate that features of the second return could not possibly apply to the first. The existence of a world-wide Diaspora of Jews is essential to the case made by the Christian Zionists, because so many of the prophecies in Isaiah, Jeremiah, Ezekiel and other prophets speak of a world-wide return of all the Jews to their ancient land to become an independent nation once again. As we examine these prophecies in Chapter 5, the reader will see how only the modern-day return of the Jews begins to fit many of these promises.

The first return from exile: the return from Babylon

We have seen earlier in the chapter that the return from the first exile was a limited return. However much one tries to widen this event, the return is described in Ezra and it consists predominantly of the people from Judah, Benjamin and the Levites (*Ezra 1:5*). At 50,000 this number was small in comparison with the numbers who had left in captivity. One Christian anti-Zionist writer (William Hendriksen) attempts to show that this return was more widespread and included those from the ten tribes of Israel and that by the time of Jesus Israel was a united nation once again.[4] In my opinion this argument is unsustainable.

Estimates put the numbers of other tribes returning at the low figure of 10-12,000.[2] What is clear is that Jewish communities had sprung up along the North African coast and around the Mediterranean from 500 BC.[5] Many remained in what is modern-day Iraq and Iran from their settlement in both the Assyrian and the Babylonian empires.[6] They formed the Jewish Diaspora well before the time of Christ. The list of Jews in Jerusalem at the time of Pentecost establishes beyond doubt that they came from all over the known world (see *Acts 2:6-11*). Yes, they were united as a people wanting to worship at the Temple, but they were in no way united as a nation back in the land. The two letters in the New Testament sent to the twelve tribes in the Dispersion (*James 1:1* and *1 Peter 1:1*) were addressed to Jewish Christians. These are likely to have been converts from the time of Pentecost who had returned to their communities and spread the word, or those who had come to faith during Paul's early missionary journeys.

What does this establish that is pertinent to an argument about the return of the Jews from two exiles?

It establishes:

1. That the nation of Israel in Jesus' time was a limited nation with inhabitants who were descendants of those who had returned from the Babylonian exile. It is quite possible that there were more Jews in the Diaspora settlements than within the boundaries of the former nation of Israel.

2. That Israel was not an independent nation. It had experienced a brief period of independence under the Maccabees,[7] but it was now a series of protectorates under the Roman Empire.

The seventy-year captivity

We have already mentioned that Judah would serve the king of Babylon for seventy years (*Jeremiah 25:8-14*). This promise is expanded in *Jeremiah Chapter 29* where the Lord explains that when the seventy years are up he will bring the people back to Jerusalem (*Jeremiah 29:10-11*). This promise is part of a long letter that Jeremiah sent to the exiles already in Babylon. The thrust of the message is that they are to accept their lot in exile and settle down there, build houses and have families. They are to pray for the welfare of Babylon because in its welfare they will find their welfare. At the end of the letter the Lord then declares his promise to bring them back to Jerusalem.

Suggested dates for this return vary. The seventy-year return could apply to any of the stages from the initial exile in 605 BC to the final stage in 586 BC. Some authors[8] put it at 516 BC which would give the seventy-year period from 586 BC, but this seems more likely to be the date at which the rebuilding of the Temple was completed (*Ezra 6:15*).

Two styles of prophecy

The two prophecies in Jeremiah are detailed, clear and business-like. They feel contemporary to the situation. There are many other prophecies which are more expansive and more poetic. While God gives information, he also expresses his heart and yearning for both Judah and Israel. As we shall see there is a strong emphasis on the two nations being brought back and brought together. It is difficult to escape the conclusion that the first return was a relatively matter of fact affair in contrast to a much wider and later return of the Jewish people to the land. The primary task of the return from Babylon was to rebuild the Temple and restore Jerusalem. No doubt this was in preparation for the First Advent of the Messiah, but it was not to create an independent nation.

In the next chapter we turn to the far more numerous prophecies which talk of a return, prophecies which cannot fit the return from Babylon.

NOTES

1.   Stephen Sizer, *Zion's Christian Soldiers* P.91 and 93.

2.   Merrill F. Unger, *Unger's Bible Dictionary* P.182

3.   The Diaspora covers the period of well over 2000 years from 586 BC to 1948 when the Jewish state was reborn as the nation of Israel. It was added to with the exile of Jews by the Romans in AD 70 and AD 135.

4.   See Article of the Month: William Hendriksen, *Are Restoration Prophecies being fulfilled Today?* Part B, *Refutation, Answer to 2:* "This is also the New Testament view. It looks upon Israel as a reunited people ...." This article is taken from: *Israel in Prophecy,* Chapter II (Grand Rapids: Baker 1968)

      <http://www.the-highway.com/articleApr04.html >

      I refute Hendriksen's thesis about the return of the Jews more fully in *Appendix 2, Section 5.*

5.   Martin Gilbert, *The Routledge Atlas of Jewish History* P.12

6.   Ibid. P.10-11

7.   See Chapter 5, Note 4.

8.   One author is Christopher Catherwood, *The Middle East* P.11. See also: Wikipedia, *Babylonian Captivity.* There are a number of articles on the timing of the 70 year captivity, which can be found in a Google search: *The Seventy year return from Babylon.* There seem no grounds whatsoever for treating this as anything other than a literal seventy years.

5 *THE SECOND RETURN FROM EXILE*

||||||||||||||||||||||||||||| ||||||||||||||||||||||||||||||||||||||||||||||||||||||||||||||||||||||||||||||||||||||||||||||

W hen we come to look at the prophecies concerning this wider return from exile there is a panoramic quality to them which is quite different from the business-like approach to the return from exile in Babylon. There is a repeated sense of the people returning from far and wide and the Lord exercising compassion. A fine example of this is the passage on the mountains of Israel (*Ezekiel 36:8-15*). These are all promises which did not find their fulfilment in the return from Babylon, the first return from exile.

God's cosmic promises

Before we proceed to examine the prophecies which relate to this later return from exile, let us look at two foundational passages in the Old Testament which to my mind are quite decisive. I have now read a mass of books and documents or excerpts from books and documents by Covenantalists which seek to demonstrate that the clear statements of the Old Testament mean something other than what they say. These two passages are so powerfully direct that I have rarely found them referred to by those who seek to reinterpret the Old Testament.

In *Jeremiah Chapter 31*, the Lord says:

Thus says the Lord, who gives the sun for light by day and the fixed order of the moon and the stars for light by night, who stirs up the sea so that its waves roar – the Lord of hosts is his name: "If the fixed order departs from before me, declares the Lord, then shall the offspring of Israel cease from being a nation

before me for ever." Thus says the Lord: "If the heavens above
can be measured, and the foundations of the earth below can
be explored, then I will cast off all the offspring of Israel for all
that they have done, declares the Lord."

(Jeremiah 31:35-37)

This promise is repeated, but in a slightly different way, in *Jeremiah 33:25-26.*

I do not see how God could have expressed his intentions with regard to Israel more clearly. Scientists tell us that if the earth departs by more than a few per cent from its orbit around the sun, then we shall all perish from the cold or the heat – it will not just be Israel which ceases to be a nation!

The second passage is King David's Song of Thanks to the Lord in *I Chronicles Chapter 16* (also repeated in *Psalm 105*):

Remember his covenant for ever, the word that he commanded
for a thousand generations, the covenant that he made with
Abraham, his sworn promise to Isaac, which he confirmed as
a statute to Jacob, as an everlasting covenant to Israel, saying,
"To you I give the land of Canaan, as your portion for an
inheritance."

(I Chronicles 16:15-18)

This passage neatly and decisively summarises the Abrahamic Covenant. It is a sworn covenant (i.e. given on oath – see *Hebrews 6:17-18*); it promises the land of Canaan to the descendants of Abraham through Isaac and Jacob, not through Ishmael or Esau. It is an everlasting covenant and in case people quibble about the meaning of everlasting, it is said to last for one thousand generations. On first reading, 1000 generations sounds a very finite number, so let us see what this means in practice. To err on the generous side let us restrict a generation to 20 years. This means a period of 20,000 years. Four thousand years or 200 generations have elapsed since Abraham's time, so we are left with another 800 generations or 16,000 years before we or the world can tell God that his covenant is up!

I hope the reader can see the problem. We either take the scriptures at face value or we say they are a metaphor: the land does not mean the land of Canaan and 1000 generations is not to be taken literally. Once we do this we lose our bearings and we seem to have a God of confusion, not least on a subject which has been of critical importance throughout history. It is especially important today when the Jews are back in the land and the Middle East is in a state of constant tension.

As we shall see in this Chapter, there are many passages which refer to a return from exile, beyond the return from the Babylonian captivity. I grant that there are a few (very few) New Testament passages which require explanation if we take the Old Testament references to the Abrahamic Covenant and the restoration of Israel literally, but these are a great deal fewer than the Old Testament passages which have to be explained if we do not take them literally. I have discovered 33 Old Testament chapters (*see Appendix 2, Section 4*) referring to a return which is different in some way from the return from Babylon. This means that the Covenantalists have to spiritualise or come up with an interpretation of each of these passages. Let us now look at the distinct features of this second return.

Distinct features of the second return

We now come to the themes which characterise this second return and make it distinct from the return from Babylon.

1. The return is worldwide; it is not just from Babylon or even from the old Assyrian and Babylonian empires.

2. The return leads to the formation of the independent nation of Israel. Israel (10 tribes) and Judah (2 tribes plus Levites) are reunited. It is no longer under colonial domination by successive empires.

3. God's restoration and blessing will be permanent. This was simply not true about the return from Babylon.

4. Israel will be strong vis à vis the surrounding nations (*Isaiah 41:8-20*). This applies to modern-day Israel, but could only be said to apply in a limited way to the Hasmonean kingdom several centuries after the return from Babylon.

5. Jerusalem will become *"a cup of staggering"* and *"a heavy stone"* for all the surrounding peoples (*Zechariah 12:2-3*). This is surely true of Jerusalem in modern times. For the Romans, Jerusalem was an irritant which it finally crushed. In no way was Rome's power weakened by this event.

6. Israel will return to the Lord and he will give them a new heart and a new spirit. This will also be a time of great blessing from the Lord. This did not happen after the return from Babylon. They returned with good intentions, but quickly fell away. The leaders and prophets like Ezra, Haggai and Nehemiah had to rekindle their enthusiasm as they laboured to rebuild, first the Temple and then Jerusalem.

It is time now to examine these prophecies of a wider return from exile, because these are the disputed prophecies. These are the ones which some writers, for example William Hendriksen, try to pack into the return from Babylon. That seems to me like squeezing a pint into a half-pint pot! Alternatively, other writers reinterpret the prophecies as no longer applying to Israel, but rather see them as applying to Christ and for the Church. (*I will examine the weakness in these two positions in Appendix 2.*)

As we examine the biblical evidence, I would ask the reader to hold in mind the theme: *God has unfinished business with the Jews as a people*, and to ask whether the evidence upholds this view.

God's promise to Israel

In the well-known passage from Jeremiah (*Jeremiah 31:31-34*) God declares that he will make a new covenant with the house of Israel and the house of Judah. This is what Christians call the New Covenant ushered in by Jesus' death on the Cross. What many Christians do not know is that this covenant was first made to the Jews in this passage from Jeremiah. It speaks of a collective transaction between God and his Jewish people. In it God promises to write his law upon their hearts. There is no way that this can yet be said to have happened to the nation as a whole. Yes, it has happened to individual Jews throughout history just as it has happened to Gentiles, but these have been few in number.

Ezekiel Chapter 37 talks about joining Ephraim and Judah as one would join two sticks. Maybe the return of Jews as a united people is the first stage in implementing this promise in Jeremiah. It is an interesting fact that right up until independence in 1948 the nation was known as 'the Hebrew State'. It was only at the last moment that the tribe name of Judah was rejected in favour of the collective name of Israel. It is my view that God worked behind the scenes to achieve this outcome.[1] This promise of a new covenant is followed in Jeremiah by the cosmic passage we have seen earlier in the chapter which underwrites the promise. As we look at these Scriptures I ask the reader to bear in mind that the modern-day return of the Jews is all about God's faithfulness, as he honours his promises in Scripture.

Worldwide return

(1) Fear not, for I am with you; I will bring your offspring from the east, and from the west I will gather you. I will say to the north, Give up, and to the south, Do not withhold; bring my sons from afar and my daughters from the end of the earth, everyone who is called by my name, whom I created for my glory, whom I formed and made.

(Isaiah 43:5-7)

*(2) In that day the Lord will extend his hand yet **a second time** to recover the remnant that remains of his people, from Assyria [Iraq], from Egypt, from Pathros [Lower Egypt], from Cush [Ethiopia], from Elam [Southern Iran], from Shinar [Southern Iraq], from Hamath [Syria] and from the coastlands of the sea [Mediterranean and beyond]. He will raise a signal for the nations and will assemble the banished of Israel, and gather the dispersed of Judah from the four corners of the earth.*

(Isaiah 11:11-12) [emphasis/comment added]

(3) Therefore thus says the Lord God: Now I will restore the fortunes of Jacob and have mercy on the whole house of Israel,

and I will be jealous for my holy name. They shall forget their shame and all the treachery they have practised against me, when they dwell securely in their land with none to make them afraid, when I have brought them back from the peoples and gathered them from their enemies' lands, and through them have vindicated my holiness in the sight of many nations. Then they shall know that I am the Lord their God, because I sent them into exile among the nations and then assembled them into their own land. **I will leave none of them remaining among the nations any more.** *And I will not hide my face any more from them, when I pour out my Spirit upon the house of Israel, declares the Lord God.*

(*Ezekiel 39:25-29*) [emphasis added]

In these passages we find a real sense of a worldwide return of the Jews from the Diaspora and this is what has happened in the twentieth century. In passage (1) we find reference to the points of the compass. The North and South are told to give them up or not to withhold them. This is what happened in the former Soviet Union; the communist regime made it very difficult for Jews to emigrate and I believe this is one reason why the regime collapsed. Immediately after the collapse in the early 1990s, Jews emigrated to Israel from Russia, the Ukraine and other former Soviet republics in their thousands. In the south Jews came from the Yemen in 1948 and from Ethiopia in the mid 1980s and again in 1991 when 14,000 Jewish immigrants were airlifted in one day.

In passage (2) we have the interesting statement that the Lord will extend his hand a second time. This is followed by a list of countries, most of which are within the boundaries of the old Assyrian and Babylonian empires, although not all of them. The reference to the coastlands (almost certainly the Mediterranean coastlands) covers the Arab countries of the North African coast. One of the consequences of the re-establishment of the state of Israel in 1948 was that the ensuing upheaval led to the expulsion of thousands of Jews from these Arab lands all over the Middle East. About 800,000 Jews either left or were expelled, and most of these were assimilated into Israel.[2]

We thus see that in the twentieth century the Jews did return once again from the Old Babylonian Empire though from a much wider dispersion than Babylon and its neighbouring cities. Just to emphasise this point the passage goes on to state that the ingathering is from *"the four corners of the earth."*

Passage (3) has one striking sentence: *"I will leave none of them remaining among the nations anymore."* This is hard to believe, but it will serve as a test of prophecy in years to come. It is an amazing fact that the Jewish population of Israel was 650,000 in 1948 and is now, 65 years later, nearly 6 million, 75% of the total population. This is still under half of the Jews worldwide. Nevertheless there are Christians who believe that the Jews will either die in the Diaspora or return to Israel as a fulfilment of this prophecy. We will have to wait and see!

An independent and unified nation

In *Ezekiel 37:15-23* God uses a metaphor of two sticks to explain how he will reunite the house of Israel with the house of Judah. He then explains the metaphor in unmistakeable terms:

> *(4) Thus says the Lord God: Behold, I am about to take the stick of Joseph (that is in the hand of Ephraim) and the tribes of Israel associated with him. And I will join with it the stick of Judah, and make them one stick, that they may be one in my hand.... then say to them [the people in exile], thus says the Lord God: Behold, I will take the people of Israel from the nations among which they have gone, and I will gather them from all around, and bring them to their own land. And I will make them one nation in the land, on the mountains of Israel. And one king shall be over them all, and they shall be no longer two nations, and no longer divided into two kingdoms.*
>
> (*Ezekiel 37:19,21-22*) [comment added]

The detail is precise. God states that Israel comprises the principal tribe, Ephraim, and the other nine tribes associated with this tribe. There is simply no way that this can be said to have happened at the time of the return from Babylon. How can a return of 10-12,000 people be said to constitute the ten tribes of Israel, when 30,000 of the tribes of Judah, Benjamin and the Levites were said to return? Even if these figures are not exact, the return from Babylon in no way reflects the grand reunion which we have just read about in *Ezekiel*.

There are many other references to Israel and Judah being reunited. See also: *Isaiah 11:12-13; Jeremiah 30:3* and *Jeremiah 31:27-28*.

In these passages we see that God will close the enmity that has existed between the two nations of Israel and Judah. They could hardly be a united and integrated nation were this not so. Some people object that modern times are so far removed from the events of exile that no one knows the tribe to which they originally belonged. We should remember that this is no problem to God. Despite intermarriage God is able to trace the descent of every person alive today, and if it matters to him, to decide which tribe predominates in their genes.[3]

A permanent restoration

God says in two passages in particular that the Jews will not again be expelled from the land. There are also other passages where this is strongly implied:

> *(5) I will restore the fortunes of my people Israel, and they shall rebuild the ruined cities and inhabit them; they shall plant vineyards and drink their wine, and they shall make gardens and eat their fruit. **I will plant them in their land, and they shall never again be uprooted out of the land that I have given them**, says the Lord your God.*
>
> (Amos 9:14-15) [emphasis added]

> *(6) You shall dwell in the land that I gave to your fathers, and you shall be my people, and I will be your God.... And I will summon the grain and make it abundant and lay no famine upon you. I will make the fruit of the tree and the increase of the field abundant, **that you may never again suffer the disgrace of famine among the nations**.*
>
> (Ezekiel 36:28-30) [emphasis added]

See also: *Joel 2:27* and *Ezekiel 36:8-15*.

To me these are the most decisive promises concerning the second return from exile. Neither of the two passages quoted, nor the two referred to, allow any possibility of this being fulfilled in the return from Babylon. It absolutely did not happen. There is simply no "wriggle room" with passages (5) and (6). After the return from Babylon they were uprooted again and they did experience famine, deprivation and persecution among the nations over two long millennia.

However, these promises are different from the passages quoted about a worldwide return of the Jews and the unification of the two nations, Judah and Israel. Those events can be witnessed in the modern state of Israel. These promises have yet to be fulfilled, but I believe time will bring that assurance.

Israel will be a strong nation

The time from the return from Babylon to the destruction of Jerusalem, a period of almost 600 years, was a time when Israel was a subject state. There was a period of about 100 years when the Maccabees established an independent state, the Hasmonean Jewish kingdom.[4] This brief period was a time of constant struggle involving attacks from outside and an eight-year civil war.

The adjective 'strong' certainly applies to modern-day Israel and it is partly this strength which antagonises so many people. We see that some of the passages referring to Israel's strength and God's protection immediately follow references to their return from across the world.

(7) I will strengthen the house of Judah and I will save the house of Joseph. I will bring them back because I have compassion on them, and they shall be as though I had not rejected them, for I am the Lord their God and I will answer them. Then Ephraim shall become like a mighty warrior, and their hearts shall be glad as with wine.

(Zechariah 10:6-7)

(8) He will raise a signal for the nations and will assemble the banished of Israel, and gather the dispersed of Judah from the four corners of the earth.... But they shall swoop down on the shoulder of the Philistines in the west, and together they shall

plunder the people of the east. They shall put out their hand
against Edom and Moab, and the Ammonites shall obey them.

(Isaiah 11:12 and 14)

Recent history demonstrates that in order to survive the hostility of
the surrounding Arab and Islamic nations Israel has had to be strong
militarily. As we saw in Chapter 1 it has had to fight several wars simply
to survive as a nation. It operates a policy of forceful response to every
attack. Western Christians find this difficult, because it feels like the
Old Testament response of *"an eye for an eye"*, rather than *"turning
the other cheek"*; but Israel does not claim to work by the principles of
the Sermon on the Mount. Neither do Western governments when it
comes to dealing with the terrorists who threaten their citizens.

Jerusalem a burden to the Nations

Many Christians do not realise how important Jerusalem is to God.
Time and again he refers to it in a very special way. Jerusalem is a
unique city. It is as though there is a living unity between the city and
its people. Two passages (from many) will convey the sense of this:

(9) I am jealous for Zion with great jealousy, and I am jealous for
her with great wrath. Thus says the Lord: I have returned to Zion
and will dwell in the midst of Jerusalem, and Jerusalem shall be
called the faithful city, and the mountain of the Lord of hosts,
the holy mountain.

(Zechariah 8:2-3)

(10) Rejoice with Jerusalem and be glad for her, all you who love
her, rejoice with her in joy, all you who mourn over her.... Behold
I will extend peace to her like a river.... So I will comfort you
[Israel]; you shall be comforted in Jerusalem.

(Isaiah 66:10, 12, 13) [comment added]

There is a sense of God hovering over his city, which makes it dangerous
for outsiders to become involved. This is illustrated most clearly in
Zechariah. At some point in history Jerusalem is going to be a great
burden to foreign nations who try to sort out its affairs. Zechariah

opens *Chapter 12* with the phrase; *"The **burden** of the word of the Lord concerning Israel"* [emphasis added]. He then proceeds:

> *(11) Behold, I am about to make Jerusalem a cup of staggering to all the surrounding peoples. The siege of Jerusalem will also be against Judah. On that day I will make Jerusalem a heavy stone for all the peoples. All who lift it will surely hurt themselves. And all the nations of the earth will gather against it.... And on that day I will seek to destroy all the nations that come against Jerusalem.*
>
> *(Zechariah 12:2-3, 9)*

Jerusalem is not referred to like this following the return from Babylon. Rome had its problems with the Jewish people in Jerusalem, but at no point was it weighed down or diminished by the city. When the time came, it dealt brutally and effectively with the city. Furthermore it was a single nation (empire). Today there are many nations all trying to intervene and arbitrate in the Middle East conflict and over the status of Jerusalem, all seemingly without success. I think we can safely say that the words of Zechariah do not apply to the destruction of Jerusalem in AD 70 and 135.

Israel will return to the Lord

We come now to the last major difference relating to the earlier return from Babylon. There are several very clear passages, principally in *Jeremiah* and *Ezekiel*, which state that the Jews as a nation will return to the Lord and as they do this they will be embraced by the new covenant that Jesus ushered in by his death and resurrection. Some passages speak bluntly about Israel no longer bringing disgrace to the name of the Lord, but others speak tenderly about God's delight in this reconciliation. He knew it would be a long time humanly speaking before it happened, but he could look down the long centuries to a time when this rift between himself and his people would be over.

At times the prophets describe the relationship between God and Israel as a marriage (*Isaiah 54:5-6*). Israel is his wife and God feels it keenly when Israel is faithless by going after other gods. *Ezekiel*

Chapter 16 talks allegorically of Jerusalem as a faithless wife. The prophet Hosea is instructed to marry a prostitute as a living testimony to God's relationship with his faithless people Israel. These verses express God's feelings:

> *(12) I made my vow to you and entered into a covenant with you, declares the Lord God, and you became mine.*
>
> *(Ezekiel 16:8)*

> *(13) Because you are precious in my eyes, and honoured, and I love you.*
>
> *(Isaiah 43:4)*

> *(14) I have loved you with an everlasting love; therefore I have continued my faithfulness to you.*
>
> *(Jeremiah 31:3)*

The pain in the prophet Ezekiel's (and therefore God's) voice is palpable as he pours forth his anger and distress at the wayward behaviour of Israel and Judah. The worship of foreign gods was not simply the pointless worship of pieces of wood and iron; it was what lay behind this. It was the worship of demonic spirits and nothing could be more offensive to God than this (*Deuteronomy 32:17; 1 Corinthians 10:19-20*).

In contrast we feel the delight in God's voice as he contemplates this spiritual reunion with his people. Let us look at two of the verses:

> *(15) For your maker is your husband.... for the Lord has called you like a wife deserted and grieved in spirit, like a wife of youth when she is cast off.... For a brief moment I deserted you, but with great compassion I will gather you. In overflowing anger for a moment I hid my face from you, but with everlasting love I will have compassion on you, says the Lord your Redeemer.*
>
> *(Isaiah 54:5,6,7-8)*

(16) And I will give you a new heart, and a new spirit I will put within you. And I will remove the heart of stone from your flesh and give you a heart of flesh. And I will put my Spirit within you, and cause you to walk in my statutes and be careful to obey my rules. You shall dwell in the land that I gave to your fathers, and you shall be my people, and I will be your God.

(Ezekiel 36:26-28)

God links this change that he will cause to happen, with blessing:

(17) I will bring them back to this place, and I will make them dwell in safety. And they shall be my people, and I will be their God. I will give them one heart and one way, that they may fear me for ever, for their own good and the good of their children after them. I will make with them an everlasting covenant, that I will not turn away from doing good to them.... I will rejoice in doing them good, and I will plant them in this land in faithfulness, with all my heart and all my soul.

(Jeremiah 32:37-41)

These prophecies of spiritual restoration to God were not fulfilled on the return from Babylon. This is so obvious when we consider the state of the nation at the time of Jesus. Some of Jesus' harshest words were spoken to the Jewish leaders, the Pharisees and the Sadducees. They had become enmeshed in the intricacies of Old Testament law, but without the love of God (see *Mark 7:6-13*).

Nor have these prophecies of a spiritual restoration yet been fulfilled in the modern state of Israel. The most that can be said is that the number of Jewish believers (Messianic Jews) has increased from 200 in 1948 to between 15-20,000 today.[5] This is still a very small proportion of the population. That these prophecies have not yet come about is a significant issue. One of the principal objections of the Covenantalists to the present return of the Jews is that they should only be back in the land when they have repented and made peace with God. There are Scriptures which are used to support this view, so I deal with this subject in *Appendix 1*.

Summing up

We have completed our review of the six significant ways in which the second return from exile differs from the return from Babylon. Now that the reader has had a chance to see some of the scriptures and to hear the arguments, let us summarise these six points:

1. The return is worldwide and includes members of all the dispersed tribes.
2. The return leads to the formation of a unified and independent nation.
3. God's restoration and blessing of Israel are to be permanent. As yet we cannot declare this to be conclusive.
4. Israel is to be a strong nation relative to its neighbours.
5. Jerusalem is to become a burden to the nations of the world.
6. Israel, as a people, is to be reconciled to God. This has not yet happened.

If I have demonstrated to the reader's satisfaction that these conditions did not prevail on the return from Babylon, **then I have demonstrated that the prophets do speak of a second, further return from exile**. The fact that this is many centuries after both the initial and the second exile is not relevant to resolving the argument, since God is outside of time. This means that the modern-day return of the Jews to the Holy Land and the establishment of the State of Israel represent this second return.

In the next chapter I wish to take a look at different ways of reading the Bible as it will help us to understand how some Christian writers allegorize Israel as the Church.

NOTES

1. Martin Gilbert, *Israel a History* P.182 and 187. Several names were proposed including: Eretz Israel (The Land of Israel), Judah, Zion and Herzliya in the days running up to the Declaration of Independence. The simple title 'Israel' was proposed by David Ben-Gurion and accepted by a majority vote of the provisional government.

2. See Chapter 1, Note 3.

3. Jewish tribes cannot be identified from modern surnames except perhaps for Cohen and Levi and their many variations. Cohen is considered to be an indicator that a person may be descended from the priesthood of Aaron, himself a descendant of Jacob's son, Levi. Cohen/Kohen means priest. The connection is acknowledged in modern times by a male Cohen being given the honour of reciting the first blessing over the Torah reading in the synagogue. The Levites were assistant priests to the Aaronic priesthood, carrying out many of the Temple's routine activities. Today they have the honour of reciting the second blessing over the Torah reading. There is a discussion of the genetic aspects of Jewishness in *Appendix 6*.

4. The Maccabees, a leading Judean family, led a revolt against the Seleucid (Syrian) King Antiochus IV Epiphanes in the Jewish Wars of Independence of 168-164 BC. They rebelled against the desecration of the Temple by Antiochus and also against the influence of Greek culture on much of the Jewish population. They re-consecrated the Temple and restored Jewish law. They established the Hasmonean dynasty which led to an independent Judean state for approximately 100 years. It was finally crushed by the Roman General Pompey in 63 BC. Despite the bravery and admirable intentions of the early Maccabees, the state became riven by feuds and civil war. It was certainly not the united state of Israel foretold by prophets such as Isaiah, Jeremiah and Ezekiel and mentioned earlier in this chapter.

   Sources: Maccabees I and II in the Old Testament Apocrypha

   Wikipedia, *Maccabees*

   Wikipedia, *Hasmonean Dynasty*

5. Estimates vary, but an idea of numbers can be gained from the anti-messianic Jewish website <http://jewishisrael.ning.com/page/statistics-1>. (If this is difficult try <http://jewishisrael.ning.com/> and go to *Missionaries in Israel* at the bottom of the web page and click on *20,000*.) The figure 200 comes from a survey carried out in 1999 by the United Christian Council in Israel. See: experts123.com and search: *How many messianic Jews are there in Israel?*

6 THE BIBLE – LITERAL AND SYMBOLIC UNDERSTANDING

Approaches to understanding the Bible

There must be a reason why two groups of Christians can come to such diametrically opposed views as to what a large part of the Old Testament means. It comes down to whether we understand the scriptures literally or whether we want to ascribe some other meaning to them: in particular to argue that some things in the Old Testament take on a different meaning in the New Testament. However, it is not as simple as this. Some of the Covenantalists, in particular Stephen Sizer, claim to read the Bible literally, but his literal understanding is clearly not the same as mine! Perhaps an examination of the Bible will help us here to resolve what is reasonably meant by 'a literal understanding of the scriptures'.

What is the Bible?

The Bible is God's Word to the human race. He has chosen to express himself through the writings of many different people. In the prophets we read the actual words that God spoke to their Jewish audiences, written down for posterity. In other writings the words are human thoughts or records of historical events. Probably most Christians, however, believe that these words have been inspired by the Holy Spirit, not least because the Bible says that about itself (see *2 Timothy 3:16* and *2 Peter 1:20-21*). It is a book about salvation and about the way we should live. It is a history book and a book about the future. It is a book of prose, but one which contains some beautiful poetry. This means that some of it is a straightforward account of both historical and future events, while other parts use literary devices such as simile, metaphor, allegory and apocalyptic symbol. Jesus himself used a special teaching device, the parable, which while not unique to the Bible, finds its most extensive use there. Parables had become an established method of teaching in the Middle East in Old Testament times.

Those who recognise this description of the Bible will also recognise that the Old and New Testaments are intimately linked, one leading into the other. We can say that the Old Testament and the New Testament form a coherent, seamless whole. The thread of salvation runs right through the Bible from Chapter 3 of *Genesis* to the end of *Revelation*.

A word of caution

For the most part the Bible can be read as a literal narrative of God's dealings with humanity. There may be issues around the dates of historical events and there are certainly gaps in the genealogies. There may be some minor contradictions in both dates and numbers, but not things which upset the literal understanding of what is being described. To give examples, the Bible's genealogies make fascinating reading, but we cannot make a complete genealogy from Adam and Eve through to Jesus Christ – the generations are said to be 'telescoped'.[1] We may read really meaningful books such as Job, but not be able to date its time in Old Testament history. One of the last kings of Judah, Jehoiachin, was described as eighteen years of age when he came to the throne in *2 Kings 24:8*, but only eight years in *2 Chronicles 36:9*, almost certainly a copying error in most Hebrew manuscripts, (the context shows that he must have been eighteen). However, these are not serious obstacles to a literal understanding of the narrative.

Nevertheless, when it comes to prophecy we do have to exercise caution, for two reasons. First of all, the prophecy does not usually have adequate information to pinpoint its future happening. However, when it has happened, it is then much easier to discern. Secondly, the language is sometimes metaphorical or allegorical. Symbolism is used instead of straight narrative. Let us examine these two points in more detail.

There are very few prophecies which are crystal clear about their future unfolding. The best example is the prophecy in Jeremiah about the return of the Jewish exiles from Babylon:

> *For thus says the Lord: When seventy years are completed for Babylon, I will visit you, and I will fulfil to you my promise and bring you back to this place.*
>
> *(Jeremiah 29:10)*

This is a clear Old Testament promise which happened as foretold. On the other hand the prophecies foretelling the birth of the future Messiah were also stated clearly, but there was no indication of the date of his arrival. These are the famous prophecies from Isaiah (*Isaiah 7:14; 9:6-7; 11:1-2*) about the birth of a child with some very special characteristics. No one anticipated the birth of Jesus, but the prophecies became clear after the event, as we know from the gospel writers.[2] The two sides in the debate of this book have no difficulty in accepting that these examples were prophecies and that they happened. Non-believers try to disparage such prophecies, but Christians believe that they have been fulfilled.

As we have already seen there are several very clear statements about a future return of the Jews to the Holy Land. They are not recognisable as metaphors or allegories. There is nothing in the text to suggest they mean something else. The question to be resolved is this: have they already happened, like the prophecies about Jesus; are they happening in the present; or are they meant to happen in the future?

Metaphors and allegories

Coming to the second point, there are however prophecies which are presented as metaphors or allegories. In some instances the metaphor is immediately explained in the text. The best example of this is the well-known story of the Valley of Dry Bones in *Ezekiel Chapter 37*. Here God uses a vivid metaphor and then tells us that *"These bones are* (in other words *represent) the whole house of Israel" (verse 11)*. The rest of the chapter then spells out very clearly, using another metaphor of the two sticks, how God will re-unite the house of Ephraim (Israel) with the house of Judah. The metaphors are vivid and the meaning quite clear. Those who would argue that the Israel referred to here (and in many other Old Testament prophecies) is a metaphor for the Church in the New Testament, have a problem to explain. Why would God use one set of metaphors whose meaning is so clearly defined and yet leave the reader to surmise that the explanation is a further metaphor? We will return to this later.

In the book of Daniel the visions given to the prophet are much more like allegories. For me an allegory is an extended metaphor or one metaphor built upon another. God introduces Daniel to four great empires in a series of visions involving 'fearsome beasts'. We are told that these beasts represent the Babylonian, the Medo-Persian and the Greek empires and that there is one to follow, more terrible that the others, which is clearly the Roman Empire. However, these visions are interspersed with references to the distant future and Daniel is told in both *Chapters 8* and *12* to seal up the visions until the end-times. Unlike the Valley of the Dry Bones God deliberately held back the explanations of some of Daniel's visions.

Where allegories, such as those of Daniel, convey the future unfolding of awesome and troubling events they are known as **apocalyptic literature**, and their metaphors as apocalyptic symbols. The most symbolic of the Bible's books is of course Revelation. From *Chapter 4* until the end, Revelation is one long apocalyptic story. However, there are still passages which speak very literally – for example the one-thousand year time-span usually known as the Millennium. However, we still have to be cautious, because the literal is mixed in with the allegorical imagery. We can surmise things, but not be dogmatic about them.

A commonsense approach

So what do I mean when I say that I read the Bible literally? I start with Derek Prince's maxim:

God means what he says, and says what he means.

If one thinks of the character of God, it could hardly be otherwise. He certainly has secrets (see *Deuteronomy 29:29*) and he sometimes veils his meaning through metaphor and allegory until he is ready to unfold it, but he does not mislead us. My guiding principle is to try to understand the scriptures literally unless it is really not possible to do so. Even where the scriptures are written as symbolic imagery, I believe it is still right to recognise that this imagery does actually represent events.

This does not mean that every word or phrase is to be taken literally. The prophets frequently use poetic language:

The wilderness and the dry land shall be glad; the desert shall rejoice and blossom like the crocus.

(*Isaiah 35:1*)

No one believes that the desert and the wilderness will behave like people, but we have no difficulty in understanding that the natural environment will respond to how it is treated. God is said to roar like a lion (*Hosea 11:10*) and Jesus is described as the *"Lion of the tribe of Judah"* (*Revelation 5:5*). The simile and metaphor respectively convey a sense of power. However, earlier in the same chapter in Hosea, we find:

... but Assyria shall be their king, because they have refused to return to me.

(*Hosea 11:5*)

No metaphor here: this is a literal prophecy and it was fulfilled when the northern kingdom of Israel went into captivity.

Another word or phrase whose literal meaning is challenged is *everlasting* and *for ever*. It is argued that it can mean *a very long time*. I agree that this is sometimes the case but certainly not always. I have looked at this much more closely in *Appendix 2, Section 3(b)*. It is a very significant issue because it is used by Covenantalists to argue that we can put a time limit on God's covenant with Abraham, Isaac and Jacob.

Summing up my approach (and that of many other Bible students) to a literal reading of the Bible, it means that I do not seek to construct a methodology for interpreting Old Testament Scriptures. I take the passages as they come, reading them literally where possible. I suspend judgement on a definitive meaning to prophecies that are written as metaphor or allegory, unless the text explains the symbolism. I exercise great caution over end-time prophecies, as yet to be fulfilled. However, where events have happened or are happening, that could be a fulfilment of prophecy, it is then quite legitimate to examine them and see how well they fit. This is my yardstick for assessing biblical prophecy. It avoids speculation, and deals with facts on the ground. This will be the approach of this book.

It is also a wise approach because it honours what Scripture itself says about prophecy:

No prophecy of Scripture is a matter of one's own interpretation, because no prophecy ever came by the impulse of man, but men moved by the Holy Spirit spoke from God.

(2 Peter 1:20-21 RSV)

Covenantalists: are they literalists?

How then does this method differ from the Covenantalists? We will spend a little time examining Stephen Sizer's approach because, unlike other Covenantalists, he makes a point of saying that he reads the Bible literally! Here are some of his statements:

One of the distinctive hallmarks of evangelicals is the way in which we seek a literal, as opposed to an allegorical

*interpretation of biblical passages. We believe that God
has revealed his purposes fully and finally in and through
the scriptures.[3]*

*Evangelicals hold to the idea of scriptural perspicuity – that
God's purposes are clear and unambiguous.*

The Bible is the very word of God.[4]

One might think from these admirable statements that Sizer is well
on the way to accepting the literal meaning of the text. However, it is
already clear that this is not what he means:

*To interpret the Bible literally is to interpret it as literature of
various kinds....*

*The goal of interpretation is to understand the meaning of
the text that the biblical writers intended to communicate
... An inspired and authoritative Bible has significance
and relevance beyond its original circumstances and
there may be many applications. **We need to work hard
at interpretation**.... So we must read the Bible literally
[emphasis added].*

The word 'literal' is a smoke screen. Sizer is as much an interpreter as
the next Covenantalist writer.

He is not what he calls an 'ultra-literalist'. He is particularly critical
with those who exercise what he calls a 'wooden literalism'. Now I
happen to think that he makes some valid criticism here, but when we
examine it we find that almost all the valid criticism relates to future
speculation. I have already indicated that such speculation is unwise.
He says:

*This error also occurs when it is claimed that contemporary
events were prophesied in the Bible such as the rise of the
European Community or Saddam Hussein's regime.[5]*

He is quite right, but that is not the same as saying that the prophesied return of the Jews cannot find its fulfilment in what has already happened in the twentieth century. I would need a microscope to find Saddam Hussein in the Bible! I certainly hold back from saying that the European Union is the revived Roman Empire. However, the return of the Jews is there for all to see. The obvious question is this: can one accept this return as the possible fulfilment of prophecy or does one have to reinterpret the prophecy, so that it does not mean or predict this return?

The essential problem for Covenantalists

Colin Chapman puts the problem very clearly. He is discussing the prophecy in Zechariah (*Zechariah 10:6-10*) which predicts the return of the Jewish exiles from both Judah and Ephraim (Israel). He argues that part of the prophecy has been fulfilled, but that part of it definitely has not. He could not put the predicament more clearly than when he says:

> *When we are faced with this kind of dilemma, we have to make a choice: either we insist that we must continue to look for a literal fulfilment in history – in which case we may see the return of the Jews to the land in the twentieth century and the establishment of the State of Israel as the intended fulfilment or we look for other ways in which these prophecies could have been fulfilled already in the past or could yet be fulfilled in the future.*[6]

Therein lies the nub of the problem for the Covenantalists. As the reader will observe when I examine examples of his writing in *Appendix 2, Section 2*, Chapman rejects a literal fulfilment and seeks an interpretation. Chapman does not claim to be a literalist, but the problem is more acute for Stephen Sizer, because he does.

Having seen that Sizer's use of the word 'literal' is rather different from mine, we find that he quickly moves on to create a methodology for interpretation. He says: we must read the Bible 'literally', 'contextually' and 'progressively'. He asks legitimate questions about the text, but immediately casts doubt on the meaning of the Old Testament words 'chosen' and 'inheritance' when examined in the light of the New Testament. This opens the door to what he calls a progressive reading of the Bible in which:

> *We usually interpret earlier passages in the light of*
> *later ones.*[7]

What we end up with is a methodology common to Covenantalists which is to interpret the Old Testament in the light of the New Testament. It is stated very plausibly and this plausibility is given further substance when at the same time Sizer highlights the inadvisability of speculating about end-time events. Colin Chapman employs a similar methodology. He devises a system for interpreting prophecy which sounds reasonable, but lacks analytical rigour and ends up with guesswork (see again *Appendix 2, Section 2*).

Examples of Covenantalist interpretation of prophecy

We are now going to list some examples of what interpretation means in practice. Since Covenantalists do not accept that modern-day Israel could be a fulfilment of prophecy, they have to change the meanings of some very fundamental words in the Old Testament. Where prophecy is concerned, words such as: 'Israel', 'Jew', 'the land', 'Jerusalem' and 'the Temple' are metaphors for something else in the New Testament:

> *(1) This is the basis for the view that the Church, made up*
> *of both Jews and Gentiles, is the successor of the promises*
> *originally made to Israel.*
>
> (Stephen Sizer)[8]

> *(2) Jesus, then, is true Israel, the one who does everything*
> *that Israel was supposed to do and who is everything that*

Israel was supposed to be. Historical Israel had failed, and the promises had not come to fulfilment through the Israelites.

(David Holwerda)[9]

(3) It seems hard to avoid the conclusion that the author views the church as the true Israel of God in which the Old Testament promises to Israel find their fulfilment.

(Wayne Grudem)[10] [commenting on Hebrews Chapter 8]

(4) When he (the apostle John) later takes up the picture of all nations attacking Jerusalem, he describes it as "the camp of God's people, the city he loves". (Revelation 20:9). This could hardly refer to the Jewish people or the city of Jerusalem and must therefore refer to the church.

(Colin Chapman)[11]

(5) The Jewish nation which rejected the offer of the Kingdom of God [was] therefore set aside as the people of God and is to be replaced by a new people.

(G. Ladd)[12]

(6) Covenantalists tend to regard promises relating to the land, Jerusalem and the temple as annulled or fulfilled in the church.

(Stephen Sizer)[13]

(7) The people of Israel living in the land had been replaced as the people of God by a universal community [the Church] which had no special territorial attachment.

(W.D. Davies)[14] [comment added]

(8) The land is still the actual land under our feet, but now it refers to the entire created earth.

(David Holwerda)[15]

*(9) Jerusalem has already expanded its borders and can
no longer be contained within the geographic limits of the
earthly city.*

(David Holwerda)[16]

Now I acknowledge that I have quoted these views without elaborating on the reasoning behind them, but they are all statements of belief which substitute something different from that which is stated in the Old Testament. (The readers will need to go to the various authors themselves if they wish to follow up their line of reasoning.)

The overarching method of interpretation

These views bring me back to constructs for interpreting Old Testament prophecy. The principal construct is to view the Old Testament through the lens of the New Testament. Lenses can change the appearance of objects and that is certainly what happens here. Although the conclusions vary slightly from writer to writer, they all arrive at a point where the promises to Israel in the Old Testament find their fulfilment in Jesus and/or the Church. I sometimes wonder whether the Covenantalists realise how many prophecies have to be subject to this process of filtering and transformation. There are many of them, especially in the major prophets of Isaiah, Jeremiah and Ezekiel. The Covenantalists make their case, frequently centred on Israel's failings in the Old Testament, but nowhere can they show that God gives a hint that these terms are a metaphor for something different in the future.

This insistence on viewing the Old Testament in the light of the New becomes a snare. At first sight it seems quite a powerful argument. Jesus is so central to the Bible story that it becomes very easy to say that the themes of the Old Testament all come together and find their fulfilment in Jesus. However, acknowledging the supremacy of Jesus does not mean transforming the meaning of words such as: 'Israel', 'Jew', 'the land', 'Jerusalem' and 'the Temple' unless:

1. The Old Testament itself indicates that while literal in the Old Testament text, they are metaphors for something else at a later date in history.

or

2. The New Testament explicitly indicates they have changed their meaning.

The only word to which the second point could possibly apply is 'temple'.

Of course, students of the New Testament are going to note the prophecies of the Old Testament which are fulfilled in the birth, life and death of Jesus. They will note too the applications of Old Testament prophecies made by the apostles themselves. They will also note passages which speak directly about the Old Testament and the effect which the New Covenant of Jesus has upon them. *Hebrews Chapter 8* is one such example and we will return to that later. However, they will not, if they are faithful to a literal understanding of the Bible, change the meaning of Scripture without an indication that God intended such a change at a later date in history.

An alternative way of comparing the Old and New Testaments

There is in my view an alternative and better way of comparing these two parts of the Bible. We keep the literal understanding of the Old Testament as far as is possible and we note whether this would create any conflict with the New Testament. Thus, for example, if one concluded that the return of the Jews means they do not need salvation like the Gentiles because God deals with them directly, then that would conflict with the New Testament and would be wrong (see *Acts 4:12*). If however, one concludes that the Jews return as a nation so that they can meet their Messiah, that would not conflict with the New Testament view of salvation and the New Covenant. Nothing in the New Testament contradicts that possibility.

Notice that with this literal approach our obligation is to search for conflict with the New Testament; not to impose an interpretation which alters the literal meaning of the prophecies, as happens when they are 'interpreted' in the light of what the New Testament has to say. The absence of conflict does not of course establish the fulfilment of the prophecies. That must be done by searching to see how they line up with what has happened in history, but it removes the red herring of trying to interpret them in the light of the New Testament. It is the simplest approach and leaves no room for dogmatic statements like this one:

> *A fulfilment in 1948 of a prophecy given by Ezekiel to people who lived in the 580s BC is thus nonsense.*
>
> (John Goldingay)[17]

Covenantalist and Christian Zionist writers

I have spent some time discussing the two different approaches to understanding the biblical prophecies concerning Israel. Before concluding this chapter I wish to say a little about the protagonists to whom I refer on both sides of this debate.

Covenantalists

It is worth reminding the reader that the Covenantalists do not believe that modern-day Israel is a fulfilment of Old Testament prophecy. They think that the Old Testament promises have found their fulfilment in Jesus Christ and/or the Church. Generally, they tend to be anti-Zionist. If the return of the Jews is not fulfilling biblical prophecy, then it is purely political and is the cause of much of the turmoil in the Middle East. However, not all Covenantalists are anti-Zionist. They stick strictly to what they think is a theological understanding of the scriptures and avoid political debate.

Three of today's best known writers are distinctly anti-Zionist:

Colin Chapman's book *Whose Promised Land?* (1983, updated in 2002) was one of the earliest to question the Christian Zionist approach to Israel. He mixes both theological and political views in an extensive coverage of the subject. He has an elaborate construct for considering Old Testament prophecies, but I think his biblical exegesis is weak and leads to false conclusions.

Gary Burge is an American professor of New Testament studies and like Colin Chapman has spent many years either in or visiting Israel and the Middle East. His particular interest is in the Palestinians and what he sees as the injustices done to them by the Israeli settlers, the IDF and the Israeli authorities. He wrote about the Middle East in the early 1990s and has more recently (2003) written *Whose Land? Whose Promise? What Christians are not being told about Israel and the Palestinians*. His knowledge of Scripture is impressive, but as with most Covenantalists he fails to distinguish properly between the Mosaic and Abrahamic covenants.

Stephen Sizer has come later on the scene, first with *Christian Zionism – Road-Map to Armageddon?* (2004), and then with *Zion's Christian Soldiers?* (2007). The first book is a partisan, but thorough account of the development of Christian Zionism in the nineteenth and twentieth centuries. I agree with some of his criticisms of dispensational Christian Zionism, but not with his conclusions about the place of Israel in God's purposes or with his attempts to play down the threats that come from Islam and Israel's enemies. The second work is more confrontational. It caused a considerable stir when first published, not least I think because he targeted Christian Zionist leaders, such as John Hagee, Tim LaHaye and Hal Lindsey. He claims to read the Bible in a literal way, but on closer examination we find his biblical exegesis is weak, both because his literalism is a cover for extensive interpretation of the Old Testament, and because he fails to separate the Mosaic and Abrahamic Covenants.

David Holwerda is another American professor of New Testament studies. He has written a theological work in *Jesus and Israel: One Covenant or Two?* (1995). Among the Covenantalists I have read, he makes the most dramatic transformation of the Old Testament promises to Israel into a fulfilment or replacement theology. He argues that the specific promises to Israel in the Old Testament have become universalized in the New Testament. Although closely argued, it is difficult to find any substantive evidence for these transformations. His writing is not political and he is not necessarily anti-Zionist.

Wayne Grudem is another respected American theologian who has written a very substantial *Systematic Theology* (1994). He is not anti-Zionist and on balance seems to believe that there will be a future large-scale conversion of the Jewish people.[18] He, like David Holwerda, is persuaded from his study of Scripture that the Church really has replaced Old Testament Israel. I hesitate to criticise such a distinguished theologian, but I again think he fails to distinguish between the Mosaic and Abrahamic Covenants when he writes about *Hebrews Chapter 8.*

William Hendriksen was another American theologian from an earlier generation. I include him because he takes a fairly unusual view among the Covenantalists in that he recognises that the Old Testament prophecies referring to Israel do mean Israel. However, he argues that they were all fulfilled in the return of the Jewish exiles from Babylon and do not therefore apply to any future return. His views were expressed in *Israel in Prophecy* (1968). His approach has the merit of taking the prophecies literally, but his thesis does not stand up, as I stated in Chapter 4. I will consider his specific arguments briefly in *Appendix 2, Section 5.*

The contribution of contemporary Palestinian Christian writers is discussed in Chapter 11, Palestinian Liberation Theology.

Christian Zionists

Just to remind the reader once again, Christian Zionists both believe that the return of the Jews to Palestine is a fulfilment of Old Testament prophecy and they support this return.

When it comes to Christian Zionist writers, there are really three categories: the popularisers of end-time prophecy, generally found in the United States; writers with a more direct interest in Israel and the Jews, often based in Britain or in Israel itself; and Bible teachers or theologians. It is worth making this distinction because Stephen Sizer targets the popularisers, people like *Hal Lindsey* who subscribe to an apocalyptic dispensationalist view of the Bible. It is easy to criticize writers who speculate about the meaning of prophecy when these speculations fail to materialise. Nevertheless, there are many serious writers about Israel who do not do this. There are people like *Murray Dixon, Sandra Teplinsky, Derek White* and *Ken Burnett,* to name but a few, who have written Scripture-based books on the Jews and the re-establishment of the State of Israel.

However, there are not many theologians, people who study and teach from the Bible as a profession. They are mostly in the other camp. The late *Derek Prince* and *David Pawson* are well-known Bible teachers, while *Ronald Diprose* is a theologian.

Derek Prince's brief, but well-argued work *The Destiny of Israel and the Church* (1992) is an excellent exegesis of the subject. Like some of the anti-Zionist writers he spent much of his life living in the Middle East. He and his family were in Jerusalem at the inauguration of the State of Israel and they lived through the War of Independence.

David Pawson is extremely well-versed in Scripture and is able to draw together the strands of God's teaching and bring them to bear on a particular subject. This the author does in relation to Israel and the covenants God makes with the human race. In my view he gives a very clear overview of these five biblical Covenants in *Defending Christian Zionism* (2008), a subject which is a source of confusion among evangelical Christians, even those well-versed in Scripture. He wrote this book in response to Stephen Sizer's second book mentioned above.

Ronald Diprose who is Academic Dean at the Instituto Biblico Evangelico Italiano in Rome, has written in depth about the origin and effects of replacement theology in *Israel and the Church* (2004).

Conclusion

I hope this chapter has given the reader an idea of how different ways of reading the scriptures can lead to very dissimilar views. Despite my respect for the Covenantalists' knowledge of Scripture and their belief in the Lord, our differences are fundamental. I believe their conclusions are wrong and that this is of vital importance to the Church. This importance, and how the Church should respond to it, will become clear in Chapter 12.

NOTES

1. See Dr. John Millam for a very full discussion of this subject in *The Genesis Genealogies: Are they complete?* <http://www.godandscience.org/youngearth/genesis_genealogies.html >

2. Simeon and the prophetess Anna, both mentioned in *Luke Chapter 2,* seemed to have foreknowledge of the birth of Christ, but that was very close to the event.

3. Stephen Sizer, *Zion's Christian Soldiers?* These quotations are all in Chapter 2, P.21-22 unless otherwise stated.

4. Ibid, P.25.

5. Ibid, P.22-23.

6. Colin Chapman, *Whose Promised Land?* P.313.

7. Stephen Sizer, *Zion's Christian Soldiers?* P.25.

8. Ibid, P.53.

9. David Holwerda, *Jesus and Israel: One Covenant or Two?* P.33.

10. Wayne Grudem, *Systematic Theology,* P.862.

11. Colin Chapman, *Whose Promised Land?* P.323.

12. G.E. Ladd quoted by Gary Burge, *Whose Land? Whose Promise?* P.177.

13. Stephen Sizer, *Zion's Christian Soldiers?* P.13.

14. W.D. Davies, quoted by Colin Chapman, *Whose Promised Land?* P.150.

15. David Holwerda, *Jesus and Israel: One Covenant or Two?* P.179.

16. Ibid, P.179.

17. John Goldingay, quoted by Colin Chapman, *Whose Promised Land?* P.317.

18. Wayne Grudem, *Systematic Theology* P.861 Foot note.

7 *COVENANT PROMISES TO THE PATRIARCHS*

||||||||||||||||||||||||||||| ||||||||||||||||||||||||||||||||||||||||||||||||||||||||||||||||||||||||||||||||||||||||||||||||||||||||||||

I hope the reader is coming to the conclusion that God's promises to Israel in the Old Testament are to be taken seriously. These promises cannot just be absorbed into a single return from Babylon nor can they be brushed away as meaning something else.

There is, however, another body of evidence which God might consider even more binding upon himself than the prophetic return of Israel to the land. I refer to his covenants. A covenant is in an altogether different league from an ordinary promise. If God swears by himself to do, or not to do, a certain thing then he has made that binding upon himself (*Psalm 89:34-35*).

We had a glimpse of this in the passage from Jeremiah (*Jeremiah 31:35-37*) where God says that if the fixed order of the sun, moon and stars can be changed, then he is not obligated to keep Israel as a nation before him for ever. This is still not a covenant, but God is posing something so contrary to our expectations of the Universe, that Israel's security as a nation is guaranteed. The only thing which is an improvement on this sort of undertaking is a covenant which God makes with human beings.

God's covenants with the human race

As I have already mentioned David Pawson gives an excellent summary on the subject of covenants in his book *Defending Christian Zionism*. A Covenant is a binding obligation, and it really is rather amazing that the Creator of the universe is willing to put himself under such binding obligations to the human race; but he does exactly this. There are in fact five covenants in Scripture in which God commits himself in this way:

◊   Noahic

◊   Abrahamic

◊   Mosaic – (the Old Covenant)

◊   Davidic

◊   Messianic – (the New Covenant)

All five are found in the Old Testament and all five can be found in the New Testament. Only the Mosaic Covenant is called 'the old covenant' and only the Messianic Covenant is called 'the new covenant'. This is because the new has superseded the old. Many times in the New Testament we are told that through the sacrificial death and resurrection of Jesus we are no longer under the ordinances of the Mosaic Law. The other three covenants have not been rescinded or replaced.

The **Noahic Covenant**, which was made through the Old Testament patriarch Noah, was the only covenant made with the whole human race (*Genesis 9:1-17*). The principal component of this covenant was that God would sustain human, animal and plant life on earth and that he would never again destroy air-breathing creatures by means of a worldwide flood. The rainbow is a reminder to God (and to us) of this covenant. Certain behaviour was required by people, but God's side of the covenant was not made conditional on this human behaviour.

The **Davidic Covenant** was the only covenant to be made with one person, King David, and the promise was that there should be a perpetual dynasty to succeed him. The ultimate successor would be the Messiah (Jesus Christ) who would occupy the throne permanently (*2 Samuel 7:1-17; Isaiah 9:7* and *Luke 1:32*).[1]

This leaves the Abrahamic, the Mosaic and the Messianic Covenants. Some writers would have us believe that because the Mosaic Law was superseded by the Messianic Covenant that the Abrahamic Covenant was also superseded. They would have us believe that the conditional nature of the promises to Israel about the occupation of the land given by Moses overrode the (virtually) unconditional nature of the promises given to Abraham. This was not so. In order to see why, we need to examine this covenant and discover its unique aspects and then observe how the Mosaic Covenant dovetails with it. We will look at the relevant scriptures in some detail.

The Abrahamic Covenant

There are several scriptures where God tells Abraham that he will give the land of Canaan to him and his descendants by Isaac. God first talks to Abraham in *Genesis Chapter 12*. He tells him to leave Haran and travel to a land he will show him and furthermore that he will make a great nation from his descendants (who incidentally will bless the world). When he and his family had arrived in Canaan God then told him (*verse 7*) that he would give this land to his offspring. By the time we reach *Chapter 15* God is describing in outline the boundaries of this land and he says this at the same time as he makes a profound covenant with Abraham.

In *Chapter 15* Abraham asks God how he is to know that he will possess this land. In response God instructs him to prepare a special sacrifice (*Genesis 15:7-11*). It then says that a deep sleep and a dreadful and great darkness fell upon him (*verse 12*). It then continues:

(1) When the sun had gone down and it was dark, behold, a smoking firepot and a flaming torch passed between these pieces. On that day the Lord made a covenant with Abram, saying, 'To your offspring I will give this land, from the river of Egypt to the great river, the river Euphrates, the land of the Kenites, the Kenizzites, the Kadmonites, the Hittites, the Perizzites, the Rephaim, the Amorites, the Canaanites, the Girgashites and the Jebusites'.

(Genesis 15:17-21)

The interesting thing about this covenant, unlike any of the others, is that God puts Abraham to sleep. All he is required to do is to prepare the sacrifice. We get no indication that Abraham is required to walk between the halves of the sacrificial animals as would normally happen. Instead a smoking firepot and a flaming torch are described as passing between the pieces. It is almost as though God is making the covenant with himself, with Abraham as a passive participant. To me, Abraham's passivity is a stark indication that God is never going to break this covenant, however Abraham or his descendants behave. It is an irrevocable covenant. The significance of God's oath is emphasised in the New Testament in the book of Hebrews (see *Hebrews 6:13-18*).

When we come to Moses' dealings with the Israelites at the end of his life we have a very clear statement that God will expel them from the land, if they do not fulfil his precepts. Its occupation is conditional, but its gift to Abraham is irrevocable. Abraham later pre-empts God by agreeing to Sarah's suggestion that he have the long-promised son by Hagar, his wife's maid, but this does not deflect God's purpose, though it does cause problems down the ages.

The nature of the covenant

Some years later in *Genesis Chapter 17* when Abraham is 99 years old God revisits him and reinforces the covenant he has already made. It is difficult to avoid the impression that God has done this in the wake of Abraham's error in trying to pre-empt God over the issue of a son. (God will not be hurried, a lesson many of us, like Abraham, learn the hard way!). There are certain, very significant features about this chapter, so we will start by quoting some passages:

> *(2) Then Abram fell on his face. And God said to him, 'Behold, my covenant is with you, and you shall be the father of a multitude of nations. No longer shall your name be called Abram, but your name shall be Abraham, for I have made you the father of a multitude of nations... And I will establish my covenant between me and you and your offspring after you throughout their generations for **an everlasting covenant**, to be God to you and to your offspring after you. And I will give to you and to your offspring after you the land of your sojournings, all the land of Canaan, for **an everlasting possession**, and I will be their God'.*
>
> (*Genesis 17:3-5, 7-8*) [emphasis added]

The first time Abraham was asleep while God made the covenant and was not required to respond in any way. This time round God requires a practical response: the mark of circumcision.

*(3) This is my covenant which you shall keep, between me and you and your offspring after you: every male among you shall be circumcised. You shall be circumcised in the flesh of your foreskins, and it shall be a sign of the covenant between me and you.... So shall my covenant be in your flesh **an everlasting covenant.***

(Genesis 17:10-11, 13) [emphasis added]

*(4) And Abraham said to God, 'Oh that Ishmael might live before you!' God said, 'No, but Sarah your wife shall bear you a son, and you shall call his name Isaac. I will establish my covenant with him as **an everlasting covenant** for his offspring after him. As for Ishmael, I have heard you; behold, I have blessed him and will make him fruitful and multiply him greatly. He shall father twelve princes, and I will make him into a great nation. But I will establish my covenant with Isaac, whom Sarah shall bear to you at this time next year'.*

(Genesis 17:18-21) [emphasis added]

In passage (2) God indicates first that the covenant is an everlasting covenant and secondly that the land of Canaan is to be an everlasting possession to his descendants. At this point there is nothing required of Abraham other than to be circumcised. This in itself is a demanding requirement because failure to implement it means the son (and possibly the father) will be cut off from his people, which probably means death (*verse 14*). There is no mention of how Abraham's descendants should behave in the land. That does not happen until the time of Moses.

Consequences of Abraham's error

At this point it is important to remember that Abraham and Sarah have upset God's plan for a nation to come forth from Abraham's loins. Instead of one line of descendants there are going to be at least two. It is a good example of God's discretionary will. He has not stopped this from happening, but his sovereign will is not to be thwarted. We see Abraham's heartfelt cry in *verse 18* that Ishmael might be the chosen descendant; but God says that is not to be: Sarah will have a son and furthermore his name shall be Isaac and it is with Isaac that the covenant will be made.

This is a crucial point when we consider the Middle East today because the Arab people lay as equal a claim to the fatherhood of Abraham as do the Jews. In passage (4) God promises to bless Ishmael and to make him a great nation, but he is quite clear that the covenant made in *Genesis Chapter 15*, reiterated and reinforced in *Genesis Chapter 17*, is with Isaac and not with Ishmael. The statement that Isaac is to be the inheritor of the covenant comes after the statement that Abraham is to be the father of a multitude of nations.

The promise to Isaac and Jacob

God went on to repeat this promise both to Isaac and Jacob. The relevant verses are found in *Genesis 26:2-5* and *28:13-15*. This is repeated in *Genesis 35:10-12* and finally relayed by Jacob to his son Joseph (*Genesis 48:3-6*).

This repetition of the promises of the covenant to Isaac and Jacob is necessary to eschew any claim to the inheritance, first by Ishmael (and Abraham's later sons by Keturah) and then by Esau, Jacob's twin brother. With this succession of the original covenant to Abraham, ratified to Isaac and then to Jacob, God unambiguously declared the covenant to operate through the twelve sons of Jacob and their descendants the Israelites. This could not be clearer. Ishmael, through no fault of his own, was conceived out of God's sovereign will and therefore not eligible for the inheritance. Esau, in contrast, did rule himself out, because he despised his birthright by selling it to Jacob.

Abraham's supreme test

I wish briefly to return to the covenant with Abraham. The supreme moment of testing in Abraham's life came with the call from God to sacrifice his son Isaac. This is one of the best known stories in the Old Testament and surely one from which all of us recoil in horror at what God asked Abraham to do. God, however, saw it differently and his response can be seen in *Genesis 22:16-18*. This passage along with the earlier passages (1) and (2) set the seal on God's promise to Abraham. God says that he has sworn by himself in response to this powerful act of obedience by Abraham. Personally, I think this passage says something about why God esteemed Abraham so highly. As we have seen, the exercise of his faith was not perfect, but the birth of Isaac must have done something for Abraham's faith from which there was no turning back.

"*God is not a man that he should lie.*" (*Numbers 23:19*). I believe that we can say on the basis of this promise alone, and without risk of being contradicted by God, that Israel has been restored as a nation in modern times to fulfil this promise. The nation and its people are still central to God's plans for this planet.

The significance of circumcision

The covenant with Abraham and his descendants is virtually unconditional; this means that it cannot be broken by God. Circumcision, which the Jews still practise, is the only requirement asked of man. The consequences for not observing this are in theory quite severe as we saw in *Genesis 17:14*. However, unlike the Mosaic Covenant, God does not say that man must keep to his side of the bargain for God to fulfil his. In this respect the Abrahamic Covenant is like the Noahic Covenant. Furthermore the only conceivable way that God could withdraw from this covenant would be for the whole Jewish people to go on strike and deny circumcision as an ordinance from God! This of course has not happened in history and will not happen now, despite modern-day attempts to ban infant circumcision![2]

To those Christians who think that circumcision speaks of the law, I would say that it is not part of the Mosaic Law and predates the law by several hundred years. It was quite a dominant issue in the New Testament when the Jewish Christians started to reach out to the Gentiles. The apostle Paul and other leaders made it clear that the practice of circumcision was not required of the Gentiles (see *Galatians 6:12* and *Acts 15:19-20*). However, because of the sensitivities of the Jews on this subject Paul arranged for his protégé Timothy to be circumcised because his mother was Jewish. His father was a Gentile (Greek) and they had not observed this Jewish rite (*Acts 16:3*).

The Abrahamic Covenant is safe for all time – it is irrevocable.

The Mosaic (Old) and Messianic (New) Covenants

God is bound by his covenant with Abraham to honour the patriarchs, and he says that he is doing this many times in Scripture, but how he honours it is up to him. We have already referred to the incident of the golden calf where God threatened to destroy the Israelites at Mount Horeb and promised to make a great nation through Moses and his descendants. Thanks to Moses' intercession this was not necessary, but had God done this he would still have been able to honour the covenant with Abraham.

We need to look at the Old and New Covenants, both of which are spoken about in the Old Testament. The Old Covenant was instituted and practised with varying degrees of success and failure – generally failure – in the Old Testament. The New Covenant was also instituted in the Old Testament, but was not realised or put into operation until the New Testament, because it depended on the death and sacrifice of Jesus.

We need to examine these two covenants to see what impact they had on the Abrahamic Covenant. Covenantalists tend to believe in one covenant[3] or at most two: the Law of Moses and the New Covenant of Jesus and they believe that the New Covenant has replaced the Old and made it invalid. We have to understand the Mosaic Covenant and also be careful to differentiate it from the Abrahamic Covenant.

David Pawson makes the point that the Old Covenant was the nearest thing that Israel had to a national constitution. It provided an overarching moral code, a set of laws and ordinances and also ceremonial procedures for the conduct of business with God and between themselves. The Israelites were about to become a nation and do the most fundamental thing that nations do, occupy territory. In contrast to all previous nations who discovered how to live together by trial and error, God was providing the Israelites with a ready-made and very detailed constitution. Furthermore, there were numerous blessings, curses and punishments depending upon how they behaved. The punishments were to be administered by themselves, but the blessings and curses depended upon God.

Furthermore, this constitution was designed to demonstrate to surrounding nations how a people connected to Almighty God should behave: that they should demonstrate mercy by making provision for the poor and needy, that their rule should be just and equitable and that they should mete out punishment for misdemeanours. It is hardly surprising that God was so angry when they failed to do this and when they adopted the ways of their sinful neighbours. They were to be a model nation.

Today, we in the West often take for granted the benign and relatively fair societies in which we live, but as we increasingly dispense with Christian values we forget that the modern democratic state based on the moral precepts of the law is the nearest thing we have to the Old Testament theocracy. Left to its own devices human society is nothing like so benign, as we have witnessed in some of the horror states of the twentieth century. Experts of various disciplines puzzle over the failure of human beings to live together more amicably in this modern age, but they forget that modern democratic states were born from Judaeo-Christian principles.

However, the failure of the Jewish nation to live by God's principles did, by default, serve another purpose. It demonstrated that sinful human nature needed a more radical solution. If direct oversight by God himself did not yield the required change, then only something as drastic as the sacrificial death of the sinless Son of God would do so.

The New Covenant: Christ's sacrificial death

The New Covenant, which as Christians we are familiar with, brought us release from the penalty for sin and gave us the new birth in Christ. It was instituted both to fulfil and to replace the Mosaic Covenant. This means that the ceremonial law and the numerous ordinances and rules, and the punishments have been superseded. Justice is still required, but it can be based on mercy.

However, the moral precepts remain. In fact Jesus raised the bar for moral behaviour in his Sermon on the Mount, but undergirded it with forgiveness and love as well as justice. Our ability to live like this has been achieved through the New Birth. However, the process of 'changing our nature' takes time and can on occasion be painful as God changes and moulds us through life's circumstances. As preachers like to say: "*we are a work in progress*".

The New Covenant in the Old Testament

What then does the Old Testament say about the New Covenant? Given that the New will supersede the Old Covenant, it not surprisingly says quite a lot, but it is important to realise that it is addressed to the Jews. Mention that the Gentiles will receive blessing through the Jews goes right back to *Genesis Chapter 12* where Abraham is told that all the families of the earth shall be blessed. The New Covenant is God's greatest blessing, first to the Jews and through them to the Gentiles.

The references to the New Covenant are in three major prophets: Jeremiah, Ezekiel and Isaiah. It is difficult to improve on David Pawson's analysis: in Jeremiah we see **what** would be the unique features of this covenant, in Ezekiel we see **how** it would be achieved and in Isaiah we see **who** would bring it about. I will leave the reader to look up these verses to see the how the New Covenant was to be implemented. As believers in Christ we have much teaching on this in the New Testament, but it is quite remarkable to see its anticipation in the Old Testament. (See *Jeremiah 31:31-34; Ezekiel 36:25-27; Isaiah 11:1-3; 7:14; 61:1-3* and *Isaiah Chapter 53.*)

There are also passages in Ezekiel where God indicates that although he is referring to individuals, he is also dealing collectively with the nations of Judah and Israel. This does not simply mean a conversion to Christ, one here and another one there, as is happening in Israel today. This is a national event. Individuals can decline this change (*Ezekiel 11:21*); it is not forced on them, but the whole tenor of the change is that it will apply to the nation as a whole. We have seen the references to this in Zechariah (*Zechariah 3:9* and *12:10-14*).

The three covenants and their requirements

For the purpose of this exercise, which is to demonstrate that the Abrahamic Covenant is still in existence, we can set aside the Noahic and Davidic Covenants. Let us summarise the demands of the three remaining covenants.

The **Abrahamic Covenant** was a virtually unconditional covenant on the part of God. God undertook to make an everlasting covenant with Abraham's descendants through the line of Isaac and Jacob and to give them the land of Canaan as an everlasting possession. He later reiterated the covenant and commanded Abraham to observe the ordinance of circumcision for himself and his descendants. There was no other requirement.

Furthermore, there was no warning that God would break his side of the agreement if the Jews were to fail to practise circumcision. There is a promise of land, but no warning that they would cease to inherit the land. Ronald Diprose sums it up by describing the Abrahamic Covenant as the: *"covenant of promise on which Israel's special identity is based".*[4]

The **Mosaic Covenant**, as we have seen, was a blueprint for law. Israel was to conduct its affairs as a nation: towards God, towards neighbouring nations and towards its own people. This covenant was highly conditional. Just about every promise was accompanied by a warning if the Israelites did not meet God's requirements. Both the blessings and warnings (*Leviticus Chapter 26* and *Deuteronomy Chapters 27* and *28*) are awesome, so much so that many Christians choose to skip over this part of the Old Testament and concentrate on the New. The ultimate warning is that if the whole nation ignores God's laws then they will be separated and expelled from the land and become subject to other nations. This is God's ultimate sanction. Thus we see that while the promise of the land is effectively unconditional, the occupation of the land is very much conditional.

The **Messianic Covenant** is like the Abrahamic Covenant. God gives much and requires very little from us as individuals, but what he does require is absolutely vital to our eternal destiny. In the New Covenant we have our sins cleansed, we are born again with a new heart and new spirit, and the Holy Spirit comes to dwell with us and guide us in our walk with God. We cannot earn this salvation, but we have to accept what Jesus has done for us.

Has the New Covenant superseded the Abrahamic Covenant?

We have seen earlier that this covenant supersedes the Mosaic Law, but the crucial question for the theme of this book is, does it supersede or in any way invalidate the Abrahamic Covenant as well as the Mosaic?

The Scripture says an emphatic "No!" The passage in Jeremiah (*Jeremiah 31:31-34*) reveals quite clearly that the covenant to be replaced is the Mosaic Covenant, the one made at the time of the Exodus from Egypt. There is no mention of the Abrahamic Covenant.

In the New Testament we find the following passage in Hebrews:

*(5) For when God made a promise to Abraham, since he had no one greater by whom to swear, he swore by himself, saying, 'Surely, I will bless you and multiply you.' And thus Abraham, having patiently waited, obtained the promise. For people swear by something greater than themselves, and in all their disputes an oath is final for confirmation. So when God desired to show more convincingly to the heirs of the promise **the unchangeable character of his purpose**, he guaranteed it with an oath, so that by two unchangeable things, in which it is impossible for God to lie, we who have fled for refuge might have a strong encouragement to hold fast to the hope set before us.*

(*Hebrews 6:13-18*) [emphasis added]

In Romans we find:

*(6) As regards the gospel, they are enemies of God for your sake. But as regards election, they are beloved for the sake of their forefathers. For the gifts and **the calling of God are irrevocable**.*

(*Romans 11:28-29*) [emphasis added]

These New Testament passages reveal that the Abrahamic Covenant is unchangeable and the call on the Jewish people is irrevocable.

It is extremely important to understand this distinction between the Mosaic and the Abrahamic covenants. Gary Burge in *Whose Land? Whose Promise?*, employs subtle arguments for justifying his change in the meaning of the promises to Israel, in particular those relating to the land, in his chapter 'Jesus and the Early Christians'. At the end he encapsulates his argument by reference to the book of Hebrews:

> In fact, the New Testament refers to previous covenants as "obsolete" and "vanishing away" (Hebrews 8:13)[5].

Burge emphasises his point with a footnote [43] which mentions two more passages, *Hebrews 7:18-19* and *9:15*, both of which clearly refer to the Mosaic Covenant. Throughout his exposition he manages to remain silent on the Hebrews passage in *Chapter 6* that actually refers to the Abrahamic Covenant (passage 5 quoted above) in which the writer emphasizes God's unchangeable promise.

Thus, an examination of all these passages in Hebrews reveals that the writer is referring to only one covenant as being obsolete, and that is the Mosaic or Old Covenant. The Abrahamic Covenant referred to in *Hebrews Chapter 6* is very much alive!

Conclusion

I think we have established in this chapter that the Abrahamic Covenant is here to stay. Covenantalists want to argue that its promises to Israel have been rescinded and that by some mysterious process, they have become a metaphor for something else. What we have seen in this chapter though, is that when God wants to warn his people that his promises may be rescinded, he does exactly that, as we saw with the Mosaic Covenant. Likewise with the New Covenant, Jesus warns his audience that those who believe in him will receive life, and those who do not will be condemned (*John 3:16-18*). This is reinforced many times by the writers of the New Testament. There is no such warning with the Abrahamic Covenant. Jews are never told that they will stop being God's chosen people or that they will cease from inheriting the land.

As we close this chapter we face a particular conundrum. How do we reconcile the promise of the possession of the land with its occupation when most of the nation has been away from the land for over 2500 years? This is an important question, because the sheer passage of time has made it difficult for contemporary students of the Bible to see any connection between Israel's re-emergence as a nation and these covenants from long ago. Let us remember, however, that time is simply no obstacle to God. We shall examine this issue in the next chapter.

NOTES

1. An abridged version of the Davidic dynasty can be followed in the genealogy of Jesus given at the beginning of Matthew's gospel. Following the deportation to Babylon, David's descendants did not rule as kings because they, as well as Israel at large, were under judgement from God. The kings, more than anyone, except perhaps the high priest, were expected to set an example. With some rare and admirable exceptions such as Jehoshaphat, Hezekiah and Josiah, the kings of Judah failed to do this. However, the promise was that an ultimate successor, the Messiah, would reign on David's throne (see also *Psalm 89:35-37*).

2. See the Jewish Chronicle 10 June 2011 for an article entitled: *Bird? Plane? Or Libel?* by Jennifer Lipman. This issue surfaces every so often – a German court ruled recently that child circumcision is illegal, this time in relation to a Muslim boy. See: BBC News Europe, 26 June 2012.

3. Stephen Sizer, *Zion's Christian Soldiers?* P.13; David Pawson, *Defending Christian Zionism*, P.44-46.

4. Ronald E. Diprose, *Israel and the Church (The origins and effects of Replacement Theology)*, P.183.

5. Gary M. Burge, *Whose Land? Whose Promise?* P.188.

8 *THE LAND*

||||||||||||||||||||||||||||||||| |||||||||||||||||||||||||||||||||||||||||||||||||||||||||||||||||||||||||||||||||||||||||||||||||

We closed the last chapter posing a problem. How could we reconcile Israel's possession of the land with its failure to occupy it?

There are two dilemmas here. One is that there seems little point in God promising the land as an everlasting possession to the people if once expelled from the land they can never again live in it as a nation. Let us remember that no conditions were attached to the promise to Abraham except the ordinance of circumcision. Possession of land may be asserted by covenant or legal document, but is usually demonstrated by occupation. Even an absentee landlord receives rent from it. This was certainly not the case for nearly 2000 years. The Jewish people were stateless and were exiles in other nations.

The other even more critical dilemma is that God must, by the very nature of his character, honour his promise to Abraham. We have seen that God very carefully reiterated the promise to Isaac and then to Jacob, so that there would be no confusion over the inheritance; but for nearly 2000 years, since the expulsion by the Romans, God does not appear to have been honouring it. If one argues, as the Covenantalists do, that God has honoured it, but has done so for and through the Church, then where does that leave the Jews as a people? It leaves them in perpetual exile.

Solving the problem

The key to solving this problem – the problem of possession without occupation – is to be found very early on in the scriptures. In fact, it is to be found before the Israelites have even entered the Promised Land and at the same time that Moses is warning them in the book of Leviticus about the possibility of being expelled from the land through rebellion and sin:

> *(1) Yet for all that, when they are in the land of their enemies, I will not spurn them, neither will I abhor them so as to destroy them utterly and break my covenant with them, for I am the Lord their God. But I will for their sake remember the covenant with their forefathers, whom I brought out of the land of Egypt in the sight of the nations, that I might be their God: I am the Lord.*
> (*Leviticus 26:44-45*; see also: *Deuteronomy 4:30*)

In both these passages God indicates that should they find themselves exiles in foreign lands, he will not utterly reject or destroy them. Furthermore, he will do this for the sake of the covenant he made with their forefathers.

In a much later passage in Ezekiel we find God returning to this theme:

> *(2) And I will vindicate the holiness of my great name, which has been profaned among the nations, and which you have profaned among them. And the nations will know that I am the Lord, declares the Lord God, when through you I vindicate my holiness before their eyes. I will take you from the nations and gather you from all the countries and bring you back into your own land.*
> (*Ezekiel 36:23-24*)

As in other passages God does not spare Israel his strictures declaring that they have profaned his name, but indicates that he will bring them back to the land, cleanse them and give them a new heart (*Ezekiel 36:26* and *29*) in order to vindicate the holiness of his name. Perhaps God considered that failure to honour his promise to the patriarchs would be seen by the other nations as profaning his name. This solution is significant because it depends on God's intent to honour his name and his promise to the patriarchs. It does not depend on Israel's behaviour in exile. We shall see its significance at a later stage when it is alleged that the Jews need first to repent before God allows them back into the land.

Ownership of the land

Before we consider the implications of this solution to the problem, let us first examine the ownership of the land. The two words used by God to define Israel's relationship to the land are 'possession' and 'inheritance'. He uses the word 'possession' three times (*Genesis 17:8; 48:4* and then *Leviticus 14:34*). In the two Genesis verses it is qualified as an everlasting possession. The word inheritance is used many times when God is telling the Israelites how they are to behave with each other and towards the people they are expelling from Canaan.

These words 'possession' and 'inheritance' might seem like outright ownership of the land, but we have to be careful here, because in several passages of Scripture God describes the land as his land:

*(3) The land shall not be sold in perpetuity, for **the land is mine**. For you are strangers and sojourners with me.*
(Leviticus 25:23) [emphasis added]

*(4) Therefore thus says the Lord God: Surely I have spoken in my hot jealousy against the rest of the nations and against all Edom, who gave **my land** to themselves as a possession with wholehearted joy and utter contempt, that they might make its pasturelands a prey.*
(Ezekiel 36:5) [emphasis added]

*(5) I will gather all the nations and bring them down to the valley of Jehoshaphat. And I will enter into judgement with them there, on behalf of my people and my heritage Israel, because they have scattered them among the nations and have divided up **my land**.*
(Joel 3:2; see also: Isaiah 14:25; Jeremiah 2:7 and Ezekiel 38:16)
[emphasis added]

One might say that this is splitting hairs: surely God owns the whole universe since he created it (*Psalm 50:10-12*), but it is difficult to avoid the impression that this piece of land is special to God and that in the present day he is about to reclaim it through his chosen people. Passages (4) and (5) indicate that God is possessive about this land. He will not have it taken by other people, nor will he allow it to be divided. Even the Israelites are not given absolute ownership of this land. There is a subtle difference between possession/inheritance and ownership. The Israelites are like *permanent tenants* who are expected to care for the land on behalf of God. The words possession and inheritance describe their relationship with other peoples who no longer have rights to the land except as sojourners. The word 'ownership' (expressed through the phrase "my land") describes God's relationship to the land. Why this land is so special to God, we can only surmise.[1]

The Israelites are thus stewards of the land and this has important consequences. It means that God is ultimately in control of the land and entitled to ask the Israelites both to behave according to his precepts and to care for the land. His instructions for resting the land in the seventh year of Sabbath rest and the fiftieth year of Jubilee were very practical (*Leviticus Chapter 25*). God reserves the right to remove them from the land, although he has made clear that the land still remains a possession and an inheritance. When they live in it and when they return to it is entirely up to God.

God, his people and his land

The whole tenor of the language about Israel in the Old Testament is one of an integral organic relationship between God, his people and his land. God is very possessive about his people. He describes them as his *heritage* (*Joel 2:17*) and in Deuteronomy he says:

> (6) For you are a people holy to the Lord your God. The Lord your God has chosen you to be a people for **his treasured possession**, out of all the peoples who are on the face of the earth. It was not because you were more in number than any other people that the Lord set his love on you and chose you, for you were the fewest of all peoples, but it is because the Lord loves you and is keeping the oath that he swore to your fathers.
> (Deuteronomy 7:6-8) [emphasis added]

However, God is also very possessive about his land. The way people behave can defile or pollute the land and this is very grievous to God. It is why he expelled the Canaanites and why he eventually expelled the Israelites.

The words 'possession' and 'inheritance' are not used about any other people in relation to the land. Yes, other peoples occupied it before Israel, and after Israel was expelled. Conquering empires (Assyrians, Babylonians, Greeks and Romans) were allowed to rule over the people of Israel and to settle their own people there, but nowhere can it be found that God made any kind of agreement in relation to the land with these other people. God made every decision about the land: he warned the Israelites through Moses that if they remained faithful to him, they would be the head and not the tail (*Deuteronomy 28:13*), but if they broke faith with him they would be the tail (*Deuteronomy 28:44*) and would be subject to other nations and empires who were in turn subject to God. It is fascinating to read of God's dealings with kings like Nebuchadnezzar and Cyrus. God spoke of Cyrus in Isaiah 150 years before he was born! (*Isaiah 45:1 and 13*).

We read in the Acts of the Apostles:

(7) And he made from one man every nation of mankind to live on all the face of the earth, having determined allotted periods and the boundaries of their dwelling place.

(Acts 17:26)

We see most clearly how this operates in the Old Testament. To say that God holds history in his hands is not some meaningless generalisation; it is a description of his active participation in history whether it was 4000 years ago, 2000 years ago or today, and this history centres on the tiny nation of Israel and that little strip of land at the eastern end of the Mediterranean.

Consequences of God's ownership of the land

Thus we have seen that the ultimate owner of the land of Israel is God; it is an ownership over and above his ownership by reason of his creation. He does not say that Africa, or the Arctic, or the moon, are his land, but he does say this about the land of Canaan. This has a very important bearing on the question of other people laying claim to absolute ownership of the land by right of having lived there for centuries. When they make this claim they are contending with God himself. They may not realise this, but when God has stated something in the Bible he does not accept lack of knowledge of his Word as an excuse for not observing it. He expects it to be transmitted by parents, teachers and spiritual mentors.

This is not about individual Arabs and Jews buying and selling land. This is foreshadowed by God in *Leviticus 25:23*. It is about outside nations laying claim to the land or attempting to prevent the nation of Israel from existing in its ancient land.

The extent of the land

Having discussed the promise of the land and its importance to God himself, it is now necessary to define the extent of this land.

In the days of the patriarchs, Moses and Joshua, there were no national boundaries such as we know them today, only the natural geographical borders like the sea, rivers or mountain ranges. We find therefore that God describes the land of Canaan by both these natural borders and by the tribes or peoples who lived within the intended land. There is an unfolding description of this territory, no doubt partly because there were at least 400 years between the original promise to Abraham and the occupation of the land. The peoples and their territory would have changed in this time. The promise, first encountered in *Genesis Chapter 12*, makes only passing reference to the land; it emphasises the promise that God will make a great nation from Abraham.

The land comes into view in *Genesis Chapter 13* when Abraham and his nephew Lot decide to separate to avoid strife between their herdsmen. Lot takes the Jordan Valley while Abraham takes the land of Canaan. God instructs Abraham to walk through the length and breadth of the land so that Abraham can see what is to be given to his descendants. The land becomes more properly defined in *Chapter 15* at the time God first makes the covenant with Abraham:

(8) On that day the Lord made a covenant with Abram [later to be Abraham], saying 'To your offspring I give this land, from

the river of Egypt to the great river, the river Euphrates, the
land of the Kenites, the Kenizzites, the Kadmonites, the Hittites,
the Perizzites, the Rephaim, the Amorites, the Canaanites, the
Girgashites and the Jebusites'.

(*Genesis 15:18-21*) [comment added]

The promise repeated to Isaac and Jacob, and later to Moses

When reiterating the promise first to Isaac and then to Jacob God does
not spell out the boundaries of the land. Instead he emphasises that
their descendants will be numerous and they will be a blessing to the
whole earth (*Genesis 26:2-5* and *28:13-15*).

God takes up the story of the land again when he talks to Moses
in front of the burning bush and describes the land as good and
broad and flowing with milk and honey (*Exodus 3:6-10*). Later when
Moses complains to God that Pharaoh has worsened the conditions
of the Hebrews, God says that he has remembered his covenant with
Abraham, Isaac and Jacob and will give them the land to possess
(*Exodus 6:2-8*). Later on God tells the Israelites that they will drive out
the inhabitants of Canaan and he sets bounds to the land: from the
Red Sea to the Mediterranean (the sea of the Philistines) and from the
Wilderness (Sinai) to the Euphrates (*Exodus 23:29-31*).

The conquest of the land

The conquest of this Promised Land takes place under Joshua who
is completely faithful to God. However, for a variety of reasons, not all
the resident tribes are driven out and this has fatal consequences for
the Israelites. Once Joshua has gone, and contrary to God's repeated
commands, they intermarry with these alien tribes and they adopt
their pagan practices. The book of Judges is all about the fortunes of
the Israelites as they ebb and flow: falling into sin, oppressed by their
enemies, repenting and then once again being restored. The failure to
conquer all the territory and drive out the inhabitants under Joshua
was not in itself a failure by the people. It was in fact ordained by
God, both for training and testing the people (*Judges 3:1-6*). Where
they failed was in succumbing to the temptations of pagan worship
and intermarriage.

Israel's supremacy in the Old Testament

The nation did not come into an enlarged territory until the time of King David and King Solomon (1 Kings 4:21). We see from the map that the kingdom extended from the Sinai desert at the Wadi el-Arish (the River of Egypt) to the Gulf of Aqaba in the south and to the River Euphrates in the north. It was bounded by the Mediterranean Sea in the west and extended well beyond the River Jordan and the Dead Sea in the east. In today's world the southern border corresponds roughly to its present-day border, but elsewhere much of Jordan, Lebanon and Syria are contained within Solomon's borders. It should be remembered that some of the surrounding states were conquered by David and made subject to Israel, but were not incorporated into the nation itself. This would have included Edom, Moab and Ammon, all in modern-day Jordan, and a large part of modern-day Syria.

The future extent of the land

The question arises as to whether Solomon's kingdom was meant to represent the full extent of the Promised Land or whether in fact it represented an empire that actually extended beyond the boundaries of Israel. Because God spoke to Abraham (Genesis 15:18) in general terms about the Promised Land stretching from the River of Egypt to the River Euphrates, confusion has arisen over what will constitute the ultimate borders of Israel. A Google search 'Boundaries of the Promised Land' reveals the range of speculation relating to these borders.

However, the two most definitive statements of the territory are given in Numbers Chapter 34 and Ezekiel Chapters 47 and 48. They appear to be remarkably similar. The borders defined by Ezekiel clearly refer to the future. Unlike the passage in Numbers, this prophecy in Ezekiel was given after the time of Solomon and these borders have never existed historically with territory allocated to the tribes as described in Chapter 48.

The problem we have today is locating certain places specified in the biblical text. However, there is very good reason to think, from the preceding chapters in Ezekiel, that this allocation of territory is to

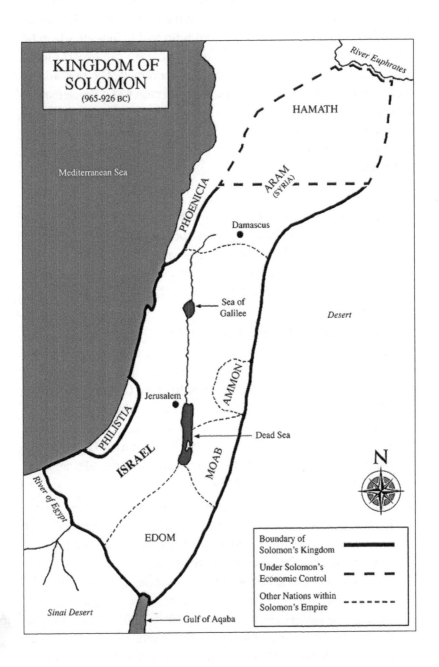

KINGDOM OF
SOLOMON
(965-926 BC)

River Euphrates

HAMATH

Mediterranean Sea

PHOENICIA

ARAM
(SYRIA)

Damascus

Sea of
Galilee

Desert

AMMON

Jerusalem

PHILISTIA

ISRAEL

MOAB

Dead Sea

N

River of Egypt

EDOM

Sinai Desert

Gulf of Aqaba

Boundary of
Solomon's Kingdom

Under Solomon's
Economic Control

Other Nations within
Solomon's Empire

apply after the ingathering of the Jewish people to the land and after the return of the Lord Jesus to earth. What may seem unclear to us now will seem very clear when the Lord is present to indicate where he wants the people of Israel to dwell. Furthermore, we can expect him to enact this with fairness to all the peoples concerned. The present day confusion over Israel's ultimate borders will cease to be problematical if the Lord himself is present.

Despite the need to be cautious about Israel's future borders I will make four observations about these borders, as described in Numbers and Ezekiel:

1. Most writers believe that the River of Egypt refers to the Wadi el-Arish (the Brook of Egypt) which runs into the Mediterranean Sea just south of Israel's current border with Egypt, and not to the River Nile. I concur with this view for the simple reason that God led the Israelites to wander in the Sinai wilderness for forty years without once telling them that this was part of the Promised Land.

2. The southern part of the Eastern border is clearly stated to run along the River Jordan from the Sea of Galilee to the Dead (Eastern) Sea. This would seem to suggest that the final drawing of the boundaries means that the tribes of Reuben, Gad and Manasseh will not return to the lands east of the Jordan which they occupied in ancient Israel. Moses allowed them to reside there, but at this stage the nation had not yet entered the Promised Land west of the River Jordan. This would also accord with the allocation of land to the tribes in *Ezekiel Chapter 48*.

3. The remainder of the Eastern border and the Northern border is more problematical. For example, the River Euphrates is not mentioned in either text, although it is mentioned several times in other, more concise descriptions. Some authors show maps with the border extending well into Syria. However, a glance at *Ezekiel Chapters 47* and *48* shows that God purposes to divide the land equally (*Ezekiel 47:14*) between the tribes starting with Dan in the North and ending with Gad in the South. This is much more practicable if the land is roughly the same width from North to South along the Mediterranean Coast.

4. Some writers discount this prophetic allocation of land in Ezekiel
    on the grounds that most Jews no longer know their tribe of origin.
    This might seem an insurmountable obstacle in the natural, but
    would be no problem to the Lord. He would be able to assign each
    Jewish male to the dominant tribe in their genetic constitution.
    (Clearly the Lord will not separate husbands and wives in this
    process!) This is another reason to believe that the Lord Jesus will
    have returned to earth when Israel's ultimate borders are put in
    place. It is premature to allegorize this passage until the world sees
    what actually happens.

*The subject of Israel's future borders highlights another area of
prophecy where it is wise to be cautious. Some writers make bold
claims for ideas which they cannot be sure of and which serve only to
raise tension on a sensitive topic. In my view it is not appropriate to
try and assess how and when Israel might come to be in possession of
land beyond its current borders. If, as already stated, Ezekiel's vision
of Israel's future borders applies to a period after the return of the
Lord, then we can expect him to be in charge.*

Israel's special association with the land

I want now to look briefly at this relationship between the Jewish
people and the Promised Land. Earlier I mentioned a kind of organic
relationship between God, the people and the land. The Bible makes
clear that the land will thrive under the stewardship of his people:

*(9) He will love you, bless you, and multiply you. He will also
bless the fruit of your womb and the fruit of your ground, your
grain and your wine and your oil, the increase of your herds and
the young of your flock, in the land that he swore to your fathers
to give you.*

(Deuteronomy 7:13; see also Deuteronomy 28:4)

This becomes even clearer when God talks about the return of the
people to the land:

(10) But you, O mountains of Israel, shall shoot forth your branches and yield your fruit to my people Israel, for they will soon come home. For behold, I am for you, and I will turn to you, and you shall be tilled and sown. And I will multiply people on you, the whole house of Israel, all of it. The cities shall be inhabited and the waste places rebuilt.

(Ezekiel 36:8-10)

(11) The wilderness and the dry land shall be glad; the desert shall rejoice and blossom like the crocus; it shall blossom abundantly and rejoice with joy and singing...

(Isaiah 35:1-2)

In *Isaiah 27:6* it says that Israel shall blossom and fill the whole world with fruit. Is this not what has happened today? It is impossible to visit Israel today and not be impressed with the cultivation of the Galilee and the Jezreel Valley.

Land can be defiled

The Bible also makes clear that sin pollutes the land and that this is highly displeasing to God. One's initial reaction might be: How can inanimate material like soil and rock possibly be defiled by sin? Nevertheless, way back at the beginning of Genesis it says that the voice of Abel's blood was crying to the Lord from the ground (*Genesis 4:10*). Before one dismisses this metaphor, let it be noted that the Old Testament refers several times to the land of Israel being defiled by the shedding of blood:

(12) You shall not pollute the land in which you live, for blood pollutes the land, and no atonement can be made for the land for the blood that is shed in it, except by the blood of the one who shed it.

(Numbers 35:33)

(13) They poured out innocent blood, the blood of their sons and daughters, whom they sacrificed to the idols of Canaan, and the land was polluted with blood.

(Psalm 106:38)

It is revealed in Leviticus that the Canaanites were to be expelled from the land because of their abominations, and in particular because of their sacrifice of children to the pagan god Molech (*Leviticus 18:21; 25-26*).

It seems that the Lord invokes these strong admonitions because he has chosen to dwell in the land among his people (*Numbers 35:34*).

Sojourners in Israel

There is one final point to address and that is God's attitude to sojourners or visitors in Israel. A series of instructions in Leviticus and Numbers make it abundantly clear that they are guests to be treated no differently from the Israelites. A passage in Leviticus (*Leviticus 25:45*) indicates that the sojourners may be part of a clan resident in Israel. They have the same privileges and responsibilities as the people of Israel. The clear implication is that the sojourner does not have to subscribe to the Jewish faith, because Scripture states (*Exodus 12:48*) that he can partake of the Passover, but only if he and all the males in his family are first circumcised. In the Bible circumcision is an important aspect of identifying with the Jewish faith.

A word of caution should be added. Welcoming a sojourner does not entail welcoming their pagan practices. Given the severity with which God warned the Israelites about idolatry and punished them for it (consider the sin of Achan in *Joshua Chapter 7*) it is unlikely that he would have tolerated such practices while they were visitors to Israel.

The Land today

So where does this leave the land and its occupation today? It should be clear by now that God is serious about bringing his people back to the land and that this is what has been happening since the First Aliyah in 1882. What is also clear is that other peoples, however long they have lived there in the last 2000 years, cannot claim God-given ownership of the land.

However, it is one thing to establish biblical principles, but another to see what this means today in practical terms. We need to be realistic about this because people's homes, livelihoods and lives are at stake.

Without getting into a discussion of Israel's recent history I will make a number of observations which I think are relevant:

1. The land was sufficiently empty at the end of the nineteenth century to sustain much larger populations of both Jews and Arabs than then existed.[2]

2. The first Jewish immigrants bought the land from Palestinian or absentee Ottoman landlords. This would seem to be God's ideal way of bringing the Jews back to the land. The reality of buying and selling the land was foreshadowed in *Leviticus 25:23* where God indicated that the land could be sold and bought, *but not in perpetuity.* Thus if Palestinians or other occupants have bought and sold land during the Diaspora, it is reasonable for the Jews to buy it back from them.

3. Land has been acquired by force of arms during Israel's War of Independence in 1948. Israel would argue that this was a consequence of Arab invasion: if the Arab states had not attacked the new nation, the Palestinians would not have lost their land.

4. The population of 20% of Arabs dwelling within the State of Israel illustrates that the Jews are observing God's requirement in relation to the Old Testament term, *sojourners.* They are permitting other peoples to dwell among them. (Some would argue that the Arabs are treated in some respects as second-class citizens in Israel. Where this is true, then it is wrong, but it is a matter that can be put right. In principle Arabs have equal democratic rights and freedom to worship in Israel, rights denied to citizens or minorities in many Arab nations.)

5. The three million Palestinians in the West Bank represent a unique challenge to Israel's moral authority. Although it was the breaking of the armistice by Jordan at the start of the 1967 war which precipitated the acquisition of the West Bank, Israel cannot escape the responsibility it now has for the resident Palestinians. Israel has been ambivalent, both in its attitude to the future of the Palestinians and towards Jewish settlement. Israel has not annexed the West Bank. It calls the land 'disputed territory' while the United Nations calls it 'occupied territory'.[3] This inevitably raises the question of whether it is right to settle in the West Bank before

the status of the territory is resolved, and whether it is right to take territory for settlement and infrastructure which is owned by Palestinians, or traditionally recognised as Palestinian communal land. The future of the Palestinians has to be addressed by Israel as well as the Palestinians themselves and the neighbouring Arab states. We should not let our theological views obscure these 'facts on the ground', just as we should not let the 'facts on the ground' obscure God's purposes for Israel. [4]

6. Since the land is ultimately God's land, he will make the decisions about who else can live there and when the full extent of its boundaries and occupation will occur. Given that we cannot discern the detail of God's plans from Scripture or his timetable for the complete re-establishment of the nation of Israel,[5] the right thing to do is to pray that his purposes will be worked out in every situation.

Sadly we know there will be conflict, both because it has happened and continues to happen and because it is foreshadowed in *Psalm 83*, a Psalm which resonates in today's world. Any nation that calls for the destruction of Israel or wishes to drive the Jews into the sea will incur God's anger – see again Passages (4) and (5).

NOTES

1. There is a view that Jerusalem may have been the location of the Garden of Eden. The possibility is mentioned, but without supporting evidence, in Sandra Teplinsky's book, *Why Care about Israel?* in the Notes to Chapter 1. (Note 3, P.255.) I am a scientist by training and I like to deal in evidence as I hope I have done throughout this book. What follows therefore is purely supposition.

    The possible connection between Jerusalem and the Garden of Eden is an intriguing idea. God has a symmetry about the way he works and it would not surprise me in the least to find that the location of man's original sin is also the location of Christ's death and resurrection to redeem the human race, and the seat of God's eventual government on earth. In the last chapter, The Church's call to pray for Israel, we shall look at the spiritual opposition to God's purposes for the Jews. This idea would go some way to explain the intensity of the conflict in the Middle East.

2. See *Appendix 3, Population Statistics.*

3. See the section in Chapter 1, *What could Israel have done differently?* Israel finally withdrew from Gaza, including its settlements, in 2005.

4. These comments are not intended to minimize the severe provocation to Israel caused by ongoing hostility from certain extremist groups and countries. However, I think it is important for supporters of Israel to recognise that the West Bank is the home of the Palestinians, some of whom have been there for a very long time. The provocations of Islamist extremists complicate matters, but it is nevertheless inaccurate and wrong to bracket all Palestinians with the extremists. Ordinary Palestinians have rights of ownership in the land and aspirations for self-determination. It is both morally and practically right that Israel should recognise this. Gaza, although intended to be part of a future Palestinian state, is slightly different now from the West Bank as Israel no longer occupies it or has settlements there. For understandable security reasons, however, Israel still exercises control over the movement of goods into and out of Gaza.

5. It is important to emphasize the uncertainty surrounding the ultimate borders of Israel. The discrepancies among the views of both religious Jews and Christian Zionists highlight this fact and remind us of the need to be cautious. See again the section, *The future extent of the land,* earlier in the chapter.

9 *ISRAEL OR THE CHURCH?*

Two people versus one

A presumption made by the Christians who wish to discount the nation of Israel is that God does not have two peoples: they argue that just as we have seen the New Covenant replacing the Old Covenant, the Church now replaces the people of Israel. Israel were the people of God; the Church now are the people of God. This argument gains strength from the fact that this transition does not exclude the Jewish people as individuals from sharing in the blessings of the New Covenant inaugurated by Jesus. They too can come to faith just like the Gentiles. However, it is considered axiomatic by the Gentile Christians that when the Jews do this they become Christians. Their Jewish past and Jewish culture are not considered relevant to the personal transaction they make with God when they accept the terms of the New Covenant. Naturally, most Jews find this very difficult. They are circumcised, steeped in their culture and united in a history of persecution. Many Jews feel bereft at being asked to leave behind their Jewishness on accepting their Jewish Messiah, Jesus, as their Saviour.

The obvious and best answer to this presumption is: "Why not? Why can God not have more than one chosen people at any one time?" Scripture certainly does not forbid it. If the motive of those who hold this view is that the idea of two peoples risks compromising the fact that salvation is found only in Christ, then this is a good motive, albeit a mistaken one. If on the other hand it derives from Church history, which early on adopted a policy of hostility to the Jews and which gave rise to replacement theology, then it is an invidious motive.

The New Covenant spelt out how salvation was to be achieved, no longer through faithful service to God, but through the atoning blood of Christ. This of necessity replaced the sacrificial ceremonies of the Old Testament, but it did not need to replace the choice of people and the promise of land in the Abrahamic Covenant, and as we have seen there is absolutely no mention that they would be replaced.

Further issues to be resolved

With the substantive weight of the evidence from prophecy and the permanent nature of the Abrahamic Covenant, one might well ask: "Is it necessary to examine further this issue of Israel versus the Church? Has not the matter already been settled?"

I would certainly like to argue this, but there are issues which still raise question marks in the minds of people. I also think it is important to deal with the subject of replacement theology: to explain its origins in the early Church and its consequences throughout Church history. It casts a shadow over the Church which is still unresolved.

The subjects to be covered in this and the next two chapters are:

◊   The meaning of the words: 'Jew', 'Israelite', 'Israel' and the 'Church'
◊   The meaning and origin of Replacement Theology
◊   The fruit of Replacement Theology
◊   Palestinian Liberation Theology

Jew, Israelite, Israel and the Church

On this subject I am greatly indebted to Derek Prince's book *The Destiny of Israel and the Church*. It is helpful to define these terms in relation to Scripture and in particular to the New Testament.

Jew and Israelite

The term Jew derived from the word Judah and originally applied to members of the tribe of Judah. After the captivity in Babylon when it was largely the tribe of Judah which returned, the word came to have a generic meaning for the people descended from the twelve tribes and the Levitical priesthood. Prior to the captivity the descendants of the twelve tribes had been called Israelites. This started with the Exodus from Egypt because up until then the Egyptians called them Hebrews. Following the return from Babylon the words 'Jew' and 'Israelite' became synonymous.

Despite the difficulties that some Jewish authorities in Israel raise in relation to being a Jew, there are only two categories of people who can be described as Jews. These are Jews of ethnic origin, by far the largest group, and those who have become Jews by conversion – in other words Gentiles who have been converted to the Jewish faith.

Much play has been made by some Covenantalists[1] that the Jews are not an ethnically pure race. This sometimes leads to the suggestion that the immigrant Jews from Russia and Europe are not truly Jews.[2] However, the Bible itself makes no secret of the fact that Gentiles married into the Jewish race. There were even Gentiles like Rahab and Ruth, who were incorporated into the Jewish nation by marriage into the royal line. They were therefore ancestors of both King David and Jesus himself. However, it is stretching credibility to argue that this had more than a marginal effect on Jewish ethnicity in biblical times.[3] Biologically, Gentile origin becomes diluted from generation to generation in a Jewish population, just as Jewish origin becomes diluted from generation to generation in a Gentile population (see *Appendix 6*).

One of the amazing things about the history of the Jews over the last 2,500 years is how they have maintained their identity as a race even when living away from Israel. Their religious and cultural identity has kept them together as an ethnic group. For much of their time in the Diaspora they have been shunned by their Gentile hosts. This in itself would have kept them apart. However, there have been times in the Diaspora such as the forced conversions to Christianity in Spain in the sixth century AD and later in the Middle Ages when Jewish identity was masked and sometimes lost through intermarriage. Even so the Marranos or Conversos, as they came to be known, still knew of and understood their Jewish origin. Today some of the descendants of these Marranos seek to have their Jewishness recognised in their desire to return to Israel.[4]

The importance of this digression is to lead us to the use of the word 'Jew' (and 'Israelite') in the New Testament. Could it possibly be that the word 'Jew' means something new, that it might now be applied to all believers, be they Jewish or Gentile? The word 'Jew' appears approximately 200 times in the New Testament and its use always means a Jew by ethnic origin. There are only three occasions where the word is used differently from its usual meaning. These are *Romans 2:28, Revelation 2:9* and *Revelation 3:9*. 'Israelite' is used in just a few instances and always with its ethnic meaning.

We will quote the Romans passage:

For no one is a Jew who is merely one outwardly, nor is circumcision outward and physical. But a Jew is one inwardly, and circumcision is a matter of the heart, by the Spirit, not by the letter.
                                                                  (Romans 2:28-29)

This is a chapter on God's righteous judgement and the fact that we will all have to stand before God to give an account of our lives (*Romans 2:16*). Paul is warning the Jews that they cannot rely on external circumcision if they break the Law, and earlier in the chapter he says:

*There will be tribulation and distress, for every human being who does evil, **the Jew first and also the Greek** [Gentile], but glory and honour and peace for everyone who does good, **the Jew first and also the Greek** [Gentile].*
                                          (Romans 2:9-10) [comment/emphasis added]

Here Paul is clearly counterpoising the ethnic Jew with the ethnic Gentile. What then is Paul doing in *Romans 2:28-29?* The important thing he is doing is to narrow down the definition of a 'Jew' to one who is not just outwardly one by circumcision, but one who is spiritually a 'Jew' by circumcision of his heart. There are simply no grounds for implying that the word 'Jew' now covers Gentiles because of the new birth. Paul could not have made the ethnic distinction clearer when he says "*the Jew first and also the Greek*". This same reasoning can be applied to the two passages in Revelation.

Three occasions out of two hundred, where the meaning of the word 'Jew' is narrowed down, are no grounds for radically changing the meaning of Scripture.

Israel

The name Israel was first used as a name change for Jacob, after he had wrestled all night with the Angel of God. It means 'having power with God'. As we have seen the descendants of Jacob were known as Hebrews in Egypt, and Israelites at the time of the Exodus. The nation came to be known as 'Israel' once the people had settled in Canaan. Following the time of Solomon, the ten northern tribes took the name of 'Israel', while Judah and Benjamin and the Levites took the name of 'Judah'. Once the exiles had returned from Babylon they resumed using the name Israel, despite most of them being from Judah. Thus, apart from the period of the two kingdoms, the Jewish nation has been synonymous with the nation of Israel and this is true today.

When we come to the New Testament, resolving the meaning of the word Israel is rather more important than resolving the meaning of the word Jew. This is because it strikes at the heart of replacement theology. Does the use of the word 'Israel' now mean that we are no longer talking about the ethnic nation of Israel, but about the Church? Has the Church become the 'New Israel'?

There are 77 occasions in the New Testament where the word 'Israel' is used, (this includes 'Israelite(s)' four times). In 75 of them the term is used with its usual ethnic meaning. Only in two of them is the word used in a special sense: *Romans 9:6-9* and *Galatians 6:15-16*. Again as we saw with the unusual use of the word 'Jew', we find the special use of the word 'Israel' restricts its use.

The Romans passage includes the following:

For not all who are descended from Israel belong to Israel, and not all are children of Abraham because they are his offspring.

(*Romans 9:6-7*)

Earlier in the chapter (*Romans 9:3-5*) Paul uses the word 'Israelite' in the normal ethnic sense. What Paul is saying in the passage quoted is that physical descent is not enough to qualify for God's promised blessing of salvation; for this they must exercise the faith of their forefathers. This is abundantly clear from the rest of the chapter. Paul starts the chapter (*verse 2*) with a heartfelt cry for his Israelite brothers and kinsmen to be saved. To him it is a tragedy that with their

Jewish heritage (*verses 4-5*) many will not be saved and we learn later (*verse 27*) that in fact only a remnant will be saved.

This chapter in no way denies the significance of the Jews or Israel once the New Covenant is in place; it simply reinforces the point I have made several times that Jews, like Gentiles, have to come to salvation through the Cross of Jesus. Later on in *Romans Chapter 11* we learn about the significance of Israel for the Gentiles and how the remnant will be saved. It also carries a severe warning about how Gentile Christians should look upon the Jews (*verses 18-24*).

In *Galatians Chapter 6* we get a use of the word 'Israel' which is used by some to justify the inclusion of Gentile believers under the umbrella 'Israel'.

> *For neither circumcision counts for anything, nor uncircumcision, but a new creation. And as for all who walk by this rule, peace and mercy be upon them, and upon the **Israel of God**.*
> (*Galatians 6:15-16*) [emphasis added]

This terminology brings out the distinction in backgrounds of Gentile and Jewish believers. The common sense approach to this passage is to recognise that Paul is talking about the importance of the new birth (new creation) and all who walk in it, namely Gentile and Jewish believers. He bestows peace and mercy on 'them' (the Gentiles) and 'the Israel of God' (the Jewish believers). Great play is made by certain writers about the connecting word in Greek, 'kai' saying that it can be translated as *even* rather than *and*. This, however, is an unusual translation. There is no call to use it here and certainly no grounds for using it as though it meant the Church. As we saw with the word 'Jew' only a tiny fraction of its use in the New Testament departs from the standard ethnic meaning of Israel.

The Church
We come now to what we mean by the Church in the New Testament. The word 'church' can mean different things to different people. It can mean a building, the worldwide congregation of all Christian churches, a particular denomination like Anglican, Baptist and Methodist or it can mean the particular church where a person belongs and worships.

New Testament Church

Most evangelical Christians know, however, that in the New Testament it has a different meaning. It means all true believers in the Lord Jesus Christ. They have acknowledged their sin and their need of salvation; they have repented of this sin and have been born again in their spirit and the Holy Spirit has come to dwell with them. They acknowledge a loving relationship with Jesus who is Lord of their life. They may well have indicated this relationship with Jesus by undergoing full immersion baptism. Several times the Bible describes Jesus as being the head of his Church (*Ephesians 5:23; Colossians 1:18*). Today these believers will be dotted all over the traditional and the evangelical churches where they meet for worship and Christian fellowship, along with others who may not yet have come into this personal faith.

The early Church was very different from the powerful institutions that later developed into the major denominations like the Catholic, Orthodox and Anglican churches. To start with it consisted entirely of Jewish believers. As time went on God revealed that it was also to be opened up to Gentiles (see the story of Cornelius in *Acts Chapter 10*). Because the majority of traditional (rabbinic) Jews rejected the gospel message, the Church began to be dominated by Gentile believers and within the space of 100-200 years it became a Gentile Church with pockets of Jewish believers. Ironically this set the scene for the development of replacement theology, though it was not in itself the cause of it. It would have been possible to have a largely Gentile Church that did not view the Jews with hostility.

The new Israel?

The New Testament is packed full with information about the Church, both its relationship to Christ as its head, the way it conducts its business and the behaviour and moral probity of its members. There are at least seven metaphors for the way Christ relates to his Church, from the Shepherd and his sheep through the Head of his many-membered body to the Bridegroom and his bride.[5] Nowhere is there a hint that the Church is now Israel or that it should be called Israel. It is clearly a new and distinct entity that has come into being as a consequence of the death and resurrection of Christ.

As we have seen there are numerous references to Jews and Israel which overwhelmingly denote their ethnic meaning. Jews and Gentiles are referred to almost as two separate ethnic groups. Yes, they are to be brought together spiritually in the new birth and ultimately to be united as one new man (*Ephesians 2:15*), but nowhere is there any diminution of their ethnic identity.

The New Testament maintains the spotlight on the Jews as God's means of bringing salvation to the world. Jesus himself said to the Samaritan woman:

> *We worship what we know, for salvation is from the Jews.*
>
> (John 4:22)

Both Jesus and the apostle Paul were frustrated at the resistance of the Jews to accepting the gospel. We have seen Paul's deep-felt anguish for the salvation of his Jewish brethren (*Romans 9:1-5*). He knows that individually, just like the Gentiles, they face a lost eternity unless they turn to God's salvation through Jesus. This anguish is not simply because, unlike him, they have not responded to this salvation, but because as a race they should have recognised that Christ was the culmination of all the blessings and history described in this passage.

> *They are Israelites, and to them belong the adoption, the glory, the covenants, the giving of the law, the worship and the promises.* **To them** *belong the patriarchs and* **from their race, according to the flesh, is the Christ** *who is God over all, blessed for ever. Amen.*
>
> (Romans 9:4-5) [emphasis added]

The apostles never once used Israel as a synonym for the Church and the phrase 'New Israel' does not occur anywhere in the New Testament.

Conclusion

Given the universal way in which the words: 'Jew', 'Israel' and the 'Church' are used in the New Testament, I think we can safely say: A Jew is a Jew, Israel is Israel and the Church is the New Testament Church. Jew and Israelite are interchangeable, but Israel and the Church most definitely are not!

Note:

As we progress to discussing replacement theology in the next chapter it is expedient to point out that I shall be using the word 'Church' both to represent believers (the New Testament meaning) and the institutions into which the Church developed, the most powerful of which was the Catholic Church based in Rome. The Church became sanctioned by the State from the time of Emperor Constantine's conversion to Christianity in AD 312. By the end of the fourth century the Christian Church had gone from being a persecuted minority faith to become the religion of the Roman Empire, a change in my opinion with few advantages and many disadvantages for its subsequent history.

NOTES

1. Stephen Sizer, *Zion's Christian Soldiers* P.46-47. Yohana Katanacho, *The Land of Christ, A Palestinian Cry* P.50-58. This is a particular emphasis of the Palestinian Christians and is dealt with more thoroughly in Chapter 11, Palestinian Liberation Theology and also in *Appendix 6*.

2. This is the thesis that the Ashkenazi Jews of northern Europe and Russia originate from the Gentile Khazar people. I deal with this in *Appendix 6*.

3. See Yohanna Katanacho, *The Land of Christ, A Palestinian Cry* P.51. He presents an extreme, and in my view, a fanciful conclusion about the Jews of Palestine being Gentile converts from the time of Esther.

4. See Website: <http://www.sephardimhope.net/>. Also Google: *Sephardim – Sleeping Giant*, an article from 5th May 2009. There are also other relevant websites.

5. The seven metaphors are (under appropriate headings):

    Salvation and the New Birth
    1. The Shepherd and the sheep
    2. The last Adam and the new creation

    Personal Growth and the Work of the Church on earth
    3. The Vine and the branches
    4. The Head and the many-membered body

    Temple, Worship and Ministry to God
    5. The Cornerstone and the stones of the building
    6. The High Priest and the kingdom of priests

    The Future
    7. The Bridegroom and the bride

10 *REPLACEMENT THEOLOGY*

||||||||||||||||||||||||||||| |||||||||||||||||||||||||||||||||||||||||||||||||||||||||||||||||||||||||||||||||||||||||||||||||||||||

One of the consequences of the Christian faith being adopted by Constantine and the Roman Empire was that replacement theology and its cousin, anti-Semitism, became institutionalised along with the Church. Covenantalists may object to the association of anti-Semitism with replacement theology, and they may argue quite reasonably that their theology has no part with modern anti-Semitism. Nevertheless, it is very important to understand that this was not so at the beginning. Anti-Semitism and replacement theology grew hand-in-hand in the early Church. It was never a neutral theology; it was always allied with contempt for the Jews.

Once the Church became a state within a state, as the Catholic Church became in Rome, it was able to enforce its religious edicts through state power, in a way that the New Testament Church never could or should have done. The most a local New Testament Church could have done would have been to exclude a person from membership and attendance of his or her local church. We see examples of this in Paul's epistles, always with an emphasis that repentance should be the preferred outcome.

Replacement theology confined to a local New Testament Church could have led to the expulsion of Jewish people, improper and undesirable as that would have been, but it would not have led to forced conversions, ethnic cleansing, badges of shame and finally murder, as happened with the state churches. We have to remember that for the best part of 1000 years (circa AD 500-1500) the Church and State were inextricably linked in many European countries. The leaders of the Church were often heads of State or wielded immense power in the secular realm.

What is Replacement Theology?

So what is replacement theology, a theology that seems to be building up a grim catalogue of charges? It is important to be clear on this because today the term 'replacement theology' can sound rather anodyne. It is simply used to express the belief which its adherents consider is grounded in Scripture, that Israel is no longer relevant to God's plans; everything is now centred on the Church.

This does have a contemporary outworking, which is that Scripture does not warrant a modern state of Israel with Jews claiming the right to return to the land. They consider that Israel's behaviour to its immediate neighbours has been wrong and that this would have been avoided if the Jews had stayed in the Diaspora. If replacement theology were a correct interpretation of Scripture, then given all that has happened in the Middle East, this might seem a reasonable "let's keep the peace" Church approach to the problem.

However, I hope that the reader will soon appreciate that replacement theology was anything but anodyne. It was grounded in a lack of Christian love which over the centuries bore some very unsavoury fruit, and bore it within the Church! With the Holocaust still fresh in our memories I think the Church has a special responsibility to examine and dispense with a theology which, however moderate it may seem today, has very ugly roots, roots which were sprouting rotten fruit as late as the twentieth century. As John the Baptist said:

Even now the axe is laid to the root of the trees. Every tree that does not bear good fruit is cut down and thrown into the fire.
(*Matthew 3:9*)

Replacement theology, or one of its variants, has become so deep-rooted in the Church over the centuries that it becomes easy to miss the connection between its origins and its fruit. Earlier I mentioned the Holocaust. When I first heard the view that the Nazi holocaust of the Jews was a natural climax to the anti-Semitism of the Church down the ages, I simply did not believe it. It seemed too awful to contemplate. After all the Nazis were criminals probably immersed in occult beliefs, not Christianity.[1]

They were extreme thugs, not men of the cloth! However, I invite the readers to see whether they agree with this conclusion, after reading the evidence!

Over time replacement theology came to represent the following views:

◊ The Jews have been disinherited in total. The covenant now belongs to the Church (Christians).

◊ The Church appropriated not only the spiritual heritage of Israel, but even the national history of the Jews, their patriarchs, prophets and men of God.

◊ The Jews are a reprobate people who rejected the prophets and crucified Jesus.

◊ Anti-Judaism led to the rise of anti-Semitism as a natural outlook of the Church.

We will come to the consequences of replacement theology later in the chapter, but in passing I mention one of the less serious, and yet almost embarrassing consequences within the Protestant Church. Certain editions of the Authorised Version of the Bible provide chapter headings at the top of the page in *Isaiah* which assign the prophetic blessings to the Church while retaining the strictures for the Jews. Thus we see headings such as these from an edition issued by the Oxford University Press: [2]

"The church is comforted" (*Isaiah Chapter 54*)

"The sins of the Jews" (*Isaiah Chapter 59*)

"The blessedness of the church" (*Isaiah Chapter 62*)

"The rejection of the Jews" (*Isaiah Chapter 65*)

"The gracious benefits of the church" (*Isaiah Chapter 66*)

Jeremiah continues with derogatory headings such as these:

"The rejection of the Jews" (*Jeremiah Chapter 15*)

"The utter ruin of the Jews" (*Jeremiah Chapter 16*)

Derek White quotes similar headings used in a version published by the Cambridge University Press.[3]

This is a selective and completely unwarranted use of allegory. It is a classic example of the Church receiving the Old Testament blessings and Israel receiving the curses, and is a good illustration of the Church appropriating what belongs to Israel!

The origin of Replacement Theology

Before we examine the fruits of this belief which came to be very serious for the Church and for the Jews, we need to study how it arose. For this study I am greatly indebted to Derek White's two booklets on the subject[4] and also to Ronald Diprose's book *Israel and the Church – the origins and effects of Replacement Theology.* This study is extremely important. Most Christians have no idea about the influence of the early Church Fathers on the Church's later attitude to the Jews. To them this is ancient history lost in the mists of time.

To begin with the Jewish Christians seemed to the majority of Jews (sometimes called *rabbinic Jews*) just like another Jewish sect and called them the 'Nazarenes'.

Two traumatic events happened in Jewish history within 100 years of Jesus' death which were bound to lead to the fracturing of the two communities, the Christian Jews and the non-Christian Jews. These events were the two Jewish revolts against the Romans. The first revolt in AD 66 led to the Jewish War in which the Jews were finally defeated in AD 70 and the Temple completely destroyed along with much of the city. The Jews surviving the siege of Jerusalem were taken captive to Rome. The second revolt was in AD 132, led by Simon Bar Kochba and finally crushed in AD 135. This time Jerusalem was ransacked. It was renamed Aelia Capitolina and rebuilt as a Roman city. Israel was renamed Syria Palaestina to remove all trace of its Jewishness. Rome had finally had enough of these rebellious Jews!

How then did this affect the relationship between the Jewish Christians and the remainder? In the first revolt the Christians refused to join the Jews in fighting the Romans. Instead they fled to Pella, east of the Jordan River in the Decapolis (in what is now

Jordan). They were no doubt responding to Jesus' call in the gospels to flee to the mountains (*Matthew 24:15-20*). However, their refusal to fight did not endear them to the Jews and they were considered traitors. When it came to the second revolt, the Christians quite understandably refused to follow its leader, Bar Kochba, whom the Jews were calling the Messiah. Not only could they not follow him, but it also dawned on them that their fellow Jews were not going to follow the true Messiah, Jesus. The sacking of Jerusalem also removed the city as the centre of the Christian Church, since Jews, which included Jewish Christians, were no longer allowed to live there.[5] This diminished the Church's influence with the Jews, as both groups had now been dispersed.

Inevitability of a schism

By this time the Christians were beginning to look on the destruction of the Temple (AD 70) and the sacking of Jerusalem (AD 135) as God's judgement on the Jewish people for rejecting Jesus, their true Messiah. Developing tensions between the two communities were not helped by the institution of a series of benedictions known as the *Birkat ha-Minim* which contained a malediction (curse) against heretics, thought to have been directed at the messianic believers among other heretics from rabbinical Judaism. This prayer may have been formulated at a Council in Jamnia circa AD 90.[6]

Thus a schism was inevitable and we know from as early as the Acts of the Apostles and Paul's writings that as the Jews resisted the gospel message and often stirred up opposition, Messianic Jews began to look outwards to the Gentiles. Nevertheless, we should not forget that many Jews in Jerusalem had come to faith. There is an interesting little passage in Acts (*Acts 21:17-20*) where Paul returning from his third missionary journey visits James, the leader of the Jerusalem church, and is told that there are many thousands of Jews who have believed, but are also zealous for the Law. Paul is advised to demonstrate by taking a vow that he also lives in observance of the Law. By contrast the instructions to the Gentile Christians in this same passage are much less demanding.

Early Church Fathers and Church writings

We find towards the end of the first century AD and into the second that Christian attitudes to the Jews and their practices were changing. As time passed, the Christian leaders came to realise that the Jewish establishment was not going to change its mind and see Jesus as the Messiah, so they began to see Jews less as converts to the gospel and more as enemies. We find quite early on that Church Fathers were describing the Jews and their practices in quite disdainful and at times intemperate terms.[7] There are several negative references to circumcision in these early writings, a practice which was particularly offensive to Greco-Roman culture.[8] Here are some examples:

Ignatius, Bishop of Antioch (AD 100-165), in his letter to the Magnesians:

> For if we still live according to the Jewish law, and the
> circumcision of the flesh, we deny that we have received
> grace.[9] ... Let us therefore no longer keep the Sabbath after
> the Jewish manner, and rejoice in days of idleness; for 'he
> that doth not work, let him not eat'.[10]

Justin Martyr from his *Dialogue with Trypho* (himself a Jew) written about AD 150:

> For circumcision according to the flesh, which is from
> Abraham, was given for a sign; that you may be separated
> from the other nations, **and from us**; and that **you
> alone may suffer that which you now justly suffer**.[11]
> [emphasis added]

The writer recognises circumcision as being from Abraham, but puts an entirely opposite value on this God-given ordinance to the Jews. By contrast the first generation of Church leaders recognised circumcision as an ordinance that was precious to the Jews.

We can find the seeds of replacement theology as early as Justin Martyr. Also in his *Dialogue with Trypho*, we find the words:

Christ is the Israel and the Jacob, even so we, who have
been quarried out from the bowels of Christ, are the true
Israelite race.[12]

Here is Origen (AD 185-254) writing in *Against Celsus*:

We may assert in utter confidence that the Jews will not
return to their earlier situation, for they have committed
the most abominable of crimes in forming this conspiracy
against the Saviour of the human race. Hence the City where
Jesus suffered was necessarily destroyed. The Jewish nation
*was driven from its country, **and another people was called***
***by God to the blessed election**... Not only was Jerusalem*
*destroyed and Israel sent into exile for crimes, **but their***
***divine election was revoked**; they were destined to stand in*
perpetual opposition to God.[13] *[emphasis added]*

For the next 300 years from the end of the first century there are
writings and a sequence of Church Fathers ending with St Augustine
(AD 354-430) who add their stamp to this negative view of the
Jewish people.

Allegories in Scripture

I want to dwell on Origen as I think he made the most significant
contribution to replacement theology among the early Church Fathers.
He was a brilliant scholar and a gifted teacher.

We have seen that underlying the idea of replacement theology is
the allegory that Scripture passages which prophesy a restoration of
Israel and its blessing actually represent the Church. This idea was
developed by several Church Fathers, but none more so than Origen
because he was the first to write a proper Christian Theology (*On
First Principles*). Origen and others grew up in Alexandria (Egypt),
the seat of Greek (Hellenist) philosophy both in the centuries
before and after the birth of Christ. They were greatly influenced by
Greek culture and philosophy, especially that of Plato (427-347 BC).

Platonic philosophy interpreted the world at three levels: the body (the literal meaning), the soul (moral and ethical meaning) and the spirit (the spiritual meaning). While Origen did not ignore the literal meaning of the Bible, he saw the deeper or allegorical meanings as more significant. The Old Testament promises thus became allegories for the Church.

As one commentator puts it:

> Origen implies that the transferral of true religion from Jews to Christians is evoked in Platonic terms, the Jews remaining trapped in the fleshly world of shadows and images, while Christians have broken through to the spiritual level. He summarises Romans Chapters 1-11 as follows: [14]
>
>> The Apostle has taught how the whole of religion was transferred from Jews to Gentiles, from circumcision to faith, from letter to spirit, from shadow to truth, from carnal to spiritual observance, and has shown that this was foretold by prophetic utterances. [15]

The seriousness of Origen's contribution is summed up by Ronald Diprose:

> His work was destined to exert great influence on the Christian approach to the Hebrew Scriptures for centuries to come.... Thus, for churchmen who read his commentaries and homilies during subsequent centuries, the idea that true Israel had always been the church appeared to be something taught by the Bible itself. [16]

If there was any lingering doubt, this was silenced by Augustine 150 years later. Like Origen he was an intellectual giant and had as great an influence on Church beliefs. His *Tract against the Jews* was one of the most influential anti-Judaic writings, and his theological writings were treated with almost canonical status by the medieval Church. [17]

An identity crisis for the Church

The reader may wonder why the allegories took the form of the Church replacing Israel, rather than some other manifestation. We have seen that by the middle of the second century AD the Church and synagogue had become separated, but this created an identity crisis for the Church. Let us remember, that at this stage it had a collection of writings: the gospels, the Acts of the Apostles and assorted letters. These were not yet collected into an accepted canon of Scripture and some went on being disputed until settled in the West by the Council of Carthage (AD 397). Up until then the canon of accepted Scripture was the Old Testament. Today we go straight to the New Testament canon to justify and establish a theology of the Church, but in the early centuries the position of the Church was theologically much less secure. As the Church began to distance itself from Israel and the Jews, it left wide open the question of a biblical foundation for the Church's existence. It is not unreasonable to hazard that this was a motivating force for the Church to argue that the Church was the true Israel *allegorically hidden* in the Old Testament, and that it had now taken over from the Jews as God's people.

Had they set contemporary Church writings against the Old Testament, they might have seen that there was room for both groups of God's people and that Israel was in fact offered a time of restoration and blessing by God, albeit at some indeterminate date in the future. There was no excuse for the Church to forbid the suggestion that the Covenant of *Jeremiah Chapter 31* included both Israel and the Church.[18] Nor was there any excuse to avoid the predictions and warnings in Paul's passage on the Jews in *Romans Chapters 9-11*. Paul's letters were considered authentic Church writing from early on.

By the end of the fourth century AD replacement theology had become a presumption of Church belief which remained largely unquestioned until the seventeenth century. How could this appalling state of affairs have arisen? We have seen some of the practical driving forces, but what of the moral dimension?

The moral failure of the early Church

Given the dreadful anti-Semitism within the Church that eventually stemmed from this early replacement theology, it is reasonable to ask: what went wrong, so terribly wrong?

This is a pertinent question because those readers who have taken for granted the idea that the Church has superseded Israel, may be saying: *"We certainly do not share or express the kinds of anti-Semitic statements made by the early Church Fathers"*. This is a perfectly valid point. As I said earlier, replacement theology may now seem quite a harmless outlook, but I also noted that its fruit has been anything but harmless.

I think at root their failure was a failure of Christian love. They had a greater responsibility in this matter than the Jews because they had the benefit of the new birth and the teachings of Jesus which the rabbinic Jews were resisting. They failed to take on board the full meaning of Jesus' teaching in the Sermon on the Mount; that his disciples should operate through love, even to loving their enemies! This must have been a tough call. Here were the majority of the Jews resisting the gospel and displaying hostility towards the followers of Christ. It is hardly surprising in the wake of the destruction of Jerusalem and the Temple, if they came to the conclusion that God had finished with the Jews. They had much more reason, with events fresh in their mind, to feel this way than we do today. Yet, surely the Holy Spirit must have tugged at their conscience when they started to use intemperate language about the Jews?

The apostle Paul's teaching

The reality is that they were wrong to speak against the Jews in the way they did, however difficult and stubborn they found them. Furthermore, they had the teaching and warning of the apostle Paul in *Romans Chapters 9 to 11*. In *Chapter 11* Paul speaks about the relationship of the Jews and Gentiles to each other within the olive tree and he warns the Gentile believers against pride. The Church Fathers either failed to recognise Paul's teaching or they failed to act on it. Ultimately they failed to exercise the love of Christ, a love that caused him to declare from the Cross:

Father, forgive them, for they know not what they do.

(Luke 23:34)

Summing up

I have spent some time examining the origin of replacement theology and the Church Fathers' responsibility for it. Apart from a few exceptions, the anti-Semitism was confined to intemperate language. However, the views expressed later paved the way and gave authority to the Church and assorted groups of nominal Christians, for example the Crusaders, to act on them. If the anti-Semitic attitudes had never been expressed, these later people would not have had a theological excuse by which to justify their actions. Consequently, the Church Fathers do carry a grave responsibility for the Church's history of anti-Semitism.

Consequences of replacement theology

I have alluded enough times to the terrible fruit of replacement theology, so it is incumbent on me to outline the Church's subsequent history in this matter.

The theology of the Church Fathers grounded the Church in an attitude of theological contempt for Israel and the Jewish people. Once the Church had become a state institution under the Emperor Constantine (AD 312), it began to enact the contempt it felt for Jews in canon and state law and to further ostracize them within society. After listing a growing number of restrictions on the Jews, enacted at various Church councils, Diprose says:

> It is clear, then, that by the seventh century Jews were, for all practical purposes, denied the privileges of citizenship. They were forced to live in what amounted to a social and legal ghetto long before the appearance of the material Jewish ghetto.[19]

In the centuries that followed, this undergirded the treatment of Jews wherever they went in the Christian world. They were stateless people, putting down roots where and when they could, but often having to move either through persecution or being forced to leave a country. For example, Edward I ordered all Jews to leave England in 1290 and they were not allowed to return until Oliver Cromwell's time 350 years later.

One cruel source of persecution was the 'Blood Libel'. These were most numerous in the twelfth to fifteenth centuries in Europe but they continued in Eastern Europe well into the 1800s. The Jews were accused at Easter/Passover time of using the blood of murdered Christian children in the baking of Passover bread. This no doubt became an excuse for the periodic pogroms of the Middle Ages. The Libel continues until this day. In 2005 twenty members of the Russian State Duma (Parliament) made a blood libel against the Jewish people, which they were later obliged to withdraw. It has found new life in the Arab media and on the 'Arab street'.[20]

Pogroms occurred at regular intervals in which the indigenous people would pillage the property of the Jews and frequently massacre the inhabitants. One particularly chilling example was the Cossack Massacres between 1648 and 1656 in Poland and Russia. They were led by Bogdan Chmielnicki and assisted by Polish peasants. Over 100,000 Jews were killed and many more tortured or ill-treated.[21] Many fled to countries in Western Europe. Pogroms were still occurring in Poland and Russia in the late nineteenth and early twentieth centuries.

Just as circumcision was considered a mark of shame from early on, the Jews were later required to wear a 'badge of shame', which eventually became the Nazis' yellow Star of David. The Fourth Lateran Council instituted such a badge to its dishonour in 1215 under Pope Innocent III in order to separate the Jews from Christians. A similar, distinctive mark was used to identify Jews in parts of medieval Islam.

One of the most significant Christians in the Church's relation with the Jews was Martin Luther. He started well, believing that with knowledge of the New Testament Scriptures and its teaching on Justification by Faith, the Jews would come to salvation. He objected to the prevailing hostile treatment of the Jews arguing *"Why should*

they convert to Christianity, when Christians treated them like dogs?"
German Jews were grateful for such sensible observations, but shared
no desire to embrace his particular theology. Later in life he turned
violently against them in his tract, *Of the Jews and their Lies* (1542).[22]
Luther's outburst meant that much of the Protestant Church inherited
the anti-Semitic beliefs of the Catholic Church. A great opportunity to
right the wrongs of over 1000 years had been missed.

More sinister, however, was that such attitudes paved the way for
Hitler and his 'Final Solution' in the twentieth century. Once Hitler
was in power (from 1933) he established concentration camps and
instituted a boycott of Jewish shops, and he said to Germany's Catholic
Cardinal Faulhaber that he was only doing what the Church itself
had been preaching and practising against the Jews. Bizarrely he had
written in *Mein Kampf* that he believed he was acting in accordance
with the will of the Almighty Creator, in warding off the Jews.[23]

It is appropriate to complete this section with a quotation from
Hans Kung, a Swiss-born theologian writing in 1974:

> *The mass murder of Jews by the Nazis was the work of
> godless criminals, but without the almost 2000-year history
> of Christian anti-Semitism it would have been impossible. The
> killing of Jews in the twentieth century was the final result of
> a tradition of denigration and rejection of Jews and Judaism
> dating from early in Christian history, which also tried to strip
> Jesus of his Jewishness to produce a home-made God and
> Saviour, a Gentile hero.[24]*

Long-term consequences for the Church

One of the sad consequences of replacement theology, with its way
of interpreting the Old Testament, is that it has made it very difficult
for Jewish people to take seriously the claim that Jesus of Nazareth is
the Messiah of Israel. Modern-day Covenantalists, no doubt keen to
take the gospel to Jews as individuals, seem unaware of the way that
replacement theology, with its parallel history of contempt for the Jews,
has made this an uphill task!

With the Reformation and the availability of the Bible to ordinary
people, the Holy Spirit was able to rekindle the spiritual life of the

Church. We find movements arising, all directed to rekindling a Church in the mould of the apostolic Church that we see described in the Acts of the Apostles. This grew enormously in the nineteenth century with the great missionary movements, but became even more dramatic in the twentieth century with the Pentecostal churches and the charismatic revival in the established churches. Today there are many movements that deliberately seek to pattern themselves on the early Church and to take the gospel across the world.

Coincidentally, this has happened at a time when awareness of what the scriptures actually say about Israel began to take root and the Zionist movement came into being. It would indeed be ironic if history demonstrates that Zionism, to which the Christian anti-Zionists are so opposed, arose because the Church began to get back to its roots, and to pray for the Jewish people to return to their ancient land, an event so literally described in the Old Testament!

Conclusion

We have seen that the Church's adoption of replacement theology, and the anti-Semitism that went with it, has cast a shadow right up to the present day. It permeated the Church's thinking. Even as late as the nineteenth century a leading evangelical Anglican minister, Bishop Lightfoot (1828-1889), could write the following in his commentary on *Mark* 13:27:

> *When Jerusalem shall be reduced to ashes, and that wicked*
> *nation cut off and rejected, then shall the Son of man send*
> *His ministers with the trumpet of the Gospel, and they shall*
> *gather His elect of the several nations, from the four corners*
> *of heaven: so that God shall not want [i.e. lack] a Church,*
> *although that ancient people of His be rejected and cast*
> *off; but that ancient Jewish Church being destroyed, a new*
> *Church shall be called out of the Gentiles.*[25]

Today the theology has become refined and has been developed with the backdrop of the Jews actually returning to the land. Covenantalists are understandably offended that they should be thought to be anti-Semitic. They make a distinction between anti-Zionism and anti-Semitism. The Holocaust shocked most people in the West, especially church people, out of any incipient anti-Semitism. Those who before the war felt there was nothing particularly unnatural about excluding Jews from the local golf club felt uncomfortable when they saw where anti-Semitism could lead.

However, the theology is still with us and the question has to be asked: Is a theology that grew hand-in-hand with anti-Semitism and yielded such dreadful fruit, a valid theology? Surely a correct theology would have yielded better fruit?

Furthermore this modern theology is not without power to influence people and change events. It undergirds Palestinian Christian thinking, one of the prime movers in modern replacement theology and it is antagonistic to the present State of Israel. This theology is helping to turn the Church at large against Israel. It is making the same mistake today as it has done all through history.

NOTES

1. Christians have no difficulty in believing that Hitler and the Nazis were motivated and driven by satanic forces. There has been much speculation on this subject, but their direct involvement in the occult has been disputed. See: Wikipedia, *Nazism and Occultism*.

2. Holy Bible (KJV), Oxford University Press. (In the author's possession: Unusually, an Impression date for this Bible is not given.)

3. As quoted by Derek White, *Replacement Theology Its Origin, History and Theology* P.16-17.

4. Derek White, *Replacement Theology Its Origin, History and Theology* and *The Root and Fruit of Replacement Theology*, both published by Christian Friends of Israel (CFI Communications).

5. See *Appendix 5, The Second Exile – Did it happen?*

6. Derek White, *The Root and Fruit of Replacement Theology* P.9-10. See also: Wikipedia, *Birkat ha-Minim*. (There is some contention about whether a Council of Jamnia took place but this is mostly in the context of whether the Old Testament canon of Scripture was finalised there. The Catholic and Protestant churches differ over which books in the Old Testament constitute its canon.) The *Birkat ha-Minim* seems to have been in place early on as Justin Martyr makes reference to a malediction in his *Dialogue with Trypho*.

7. Translations of all the early Church Fathers' writings can be found at the website: <http://www.earlychristianwritings.com>. This is a massive resource, designed for researchers. The quotations I use will generally be referenced to the authors I have used.

8. *History of Circumcision* <http://www.cirp.org/library/history/#n34>. CIRP is the acronym for *Circumcision Information Resource Pages* on the Worldwide Web.

9. *Letter to the Magnesians.* Scroll down to Chapter VIII – Caution Against False Doctrines. <http://www.earlychristianwritings.com/text/ignatius-magnesians-longer.html>.

10. Ibid. Chapter IX – Let Us Live with Christ

11. Derek White, *The Root and Fruit of Replacement Theology* P.19. (Quoting from: N.R. Needham, *2000 years of Christ's Power* Vol.1 Grace Publications 1996 P.85-87.)

12. Ibid. P.18.

13. Ibid. P.28 (Origen, *Against Celsus* Book IV Ch.22f, cited in *Ante-nicene Christian Literature* Vol.IV P.506.)

14. Joseph S. O'Leary Home Page. *Origen on Judaism* Enter website <http://josephsoleary.typepad.com/my_weblog/> Scroll down the Categories column and click on Origen. Then scroll down to *Origen on Judaism* Para 4.

15. Ibid. Scroll down to *The Recuperation of Judaism* Para.6.

16. Ronald E. Diprose, *Israel and the Church, The Origin and Effects of Replacement Theology* P.82 and 87.

17. Derek White, *The Root and Fruit of Replacement Theology* P.30.

18. Derek White, *Replacement Theology Its Origin, History and Theology* P.7.

19. Ronald E. Diprose, *Israel and the Church, The Origin and Effects of Replacement Theology* P.95.

20. Wikipedia, *Blood Libel.* Section: 20th Century and Beyond. Also: <http://www.aish.com/> Search *Blood Libels – Yesterday and Today.*

21. Max Dimont, *Jews, God and History* P.228, 230, 245-246. Martin Gilbert, *The Routledge Atlas of Jewish History* P.56.

22. Derek White, *Replacement Theology Its Origin, History and Theology* P.9-10, (citing: Martin Luther, *Antisemitism,* Encyclopaedia Judaica).

23. Ibid. P.10.

24. Ibid. P.10 (citing: Hans Kung, The Times, April 1985).

25. Derek White, *Replacement Theology Its Origin, History and Theology* P.17.

11 *PALESTINIAN LIBERATION THEOLOGY*

B efore looking into the subject of Palestinian liberation theology it is worth explaining the demographics of faith in Israel and the Palestinian territories. The Jewish population in Israel is largely secular. Around 70% subscribe to no faith while the remainder range from some affinity with the Jewish faith to strictly orthodox belief. The Arabs in the West Bank are largely Muslim (circa 90%) or nominally Christian. The Christians belong mainly to the Catholic or Greek Orthodox churches. These figures are mirrored for Arabs living within Israel. In Gaza over 99% are Muslims.[1]

The number of evangelical Christians, those with a personal faith in Jesus Christ, represents only a tiny part of the population of Jews in Israel and Arabs in the Palestinian territories. Sadly, the conflict between Jews and Arabs in the Middle East tends to be mirrored by these two groups of evangelical believers. They are brothers and sisters in Christ, but each side views the other with suspicion. The Messianic believers (Jewish Christians) think that the Palestinians do not understand God's purposes in restoring the Jews to their ancient land, while Palestinian Christians think that the Messianic believers close their eyes to what they perceive as the injustices of the State of Israel towards the Palestinians.[2]

Christ at the Checkpoint conference

It was in this context in March 2012 that my wife and I decided to attend a conference in Bethlehem called 'Christ at the Checkpoint'. This was a conference organised by the Bethlehem Bible College to highlight the difficulties of the Palestinians in the West Bank and Gaza, and to present a biblical challenge to Christian Zionism and its support for the State of Israel. In deciding to attend we had three things in mind. We wanted to see what it was actually like for ordinary Palestinians living in the West Bank; we wanted to learn about their theological approach to Israel first hand and we wanted to see what steps were being taken to bring reconciliation between these two groups of believers in Jesus, across the Middle East divide. We felt, before we went, that it was on God's heart to see reconciliation between these two sets of believers.

We could see for ourselves that ordinary Palestinians are suffering in their daily lives. It serves no useful purpose for Christian supporters of Israel to deny this or to minimize its significance. We could also see that the history of the Middle East conflict has caused Palestinian Christian leaders to arrive at a very different, and in our view, mistaken understanding of what the scriptures have to say about God's purposes for Israel. Their theology has become entangled with their politics. On the subject of reconciliation we were encouraged by the tentative steps which have been taken behind the scenes for dialogue and fellowship between the leaders of Messianic and Palestinian congregations. In some cases this has been going on for a number of years.

The conference met with suspicion and opposition by Messianic fellowships and Christian Zionists before it took place. Many Palestinian speakers aired their grievances about Israel in ways which reinforced these suspicions. However, the conference leaders had invited Messianic leaders to attend and some of these were invited to speak. It was from these and a few Palestinian counterparts that we learnt of the real efforts at reconciliation. Some of their contributions were genuinely moving. Reconciliation requires recognition of faults on both sides of the Middle East divide; it requires forgiveness and above all it requires courage and humility. A Palestinian Christian who goes too openly down the path of reconciliation puts his life at risk.[3] A Messianic believer who espouses the same cause risks severe disapproval from the Messianic community. Nevertheless, we felt that reconciliation is what God is seeking.

The conference did not shift our views about the place of Israel in God's purposes. These remain firmly grounded in the Bible. However, having met many people at the conference and seen the deep anger felt towards Israel's treatment of the Palestinians, we do not expect the Palestinian Christians to see the biblical case for Israel straight away. We think it is unrealistic of Christian supporters of Israel to expect otherwise. The way forward on this is for an extension of the fellowship that has already happened, in which the two sides agree to respect their differences, but work and pray together for the furtherance of God's kingdom among unbelieving Jews and Palestinians. It was moving to see one Palestinian speaker testify how God had changed his heart from a lifelong hatred of the Jews to one of love for them.

Who are the evangelical Palestinian Christians?

The evangelical Palestinian Christians are a very small minority of the population and even of the official Christian churches, numbering perhaps a few hundred.[4] They feel, and are, very isolated – pressured by Israel because they are Palestinians and pressured by the Palestinian authorities because they are neither Muslims nor do they belong to the recognised churches, Catholic and Greek Orthodox. Functions of the state such as social security, birth and marriage certificates all have to be handled through an official religious body such as a mosque or recognised church. Evangelical churches may not be recognised and this can make life very hard for their members. Furthermore they are isolated from the many Christians in the West who support and visit Israel, but do not even know that evangelical Christians exist in the West Bank and Gaza.

For me the most enduring memory of the Christ at the Checkpoint conference was the leader who said, *"Come and see us. You do not have to accept our theology. Just come and visit us."*

This is reiterated by Naim Ateek:

> *Christian Zionists do not relate to Palestinian Christians at all. Thousands of Christian Zionists visit Israel every year. They do not go into the West Bank or visit people there.*[5]

Palestinian Liberation Theology

Palestinian liberation theology has grown out of the experience of
Palestinian Christians in their daily lives under Israeli occupation. This
theology is similar to, but not identical with, replacement theology.
Their experience of occupation has led them to doubt that Israel's
restoration in the twentieth century has anything to do with God's
purposes and is thus in stark contrast to the Christian Zionist view.
Although I sympathize with the situation of the Palestinian Christians,
I think it is important to challenge their theology.

There are three principal Palestinian theologians: Canon Naim Ateek,
Rev Mitri Raheb and Rev Yohanna Katanacho. Ateek is a Palestinian
citizen of Israel who experienced Israel's War of Independence in a very
direct and traumatic way. He is really the father of Palestinian liberation
theology with his book *Justice and Only Justice: A Palestinian Theology of
Liberation* written in 1989 at the height of the First Intifada. More recently
he has written *A Palestinian Christian Cry for Reconciliation*. Raheb is a
Palestinian whose family has long lived in Bethlehem and has written *I
am a Palestinian Christian*, while Katanacho is the author of *The Land
of Christ, a Palestinian Cry*. He has been associated with the publication
of *The Kairos Palestine Document*. This was published in 2009 and
presented a combined Palestinian Church view of the situation in the
West Bank and Gaza in both a political and a theological context.[6]

The Kairos document has received much sympathetic attention
from the World Council of Churches (WCC). Many mainline churches
in the West now support the Palestinian Christians in their difficult
situation. This is perfectly understandable, but I believe it should be
possible to do this without discarding a biblical understanding of the
place of Israel in God's purposes. However, the Palestinian Christians
and the WCC do not see it this way.

There are two main aspects to their theology. The first is their
emphasis on God's message of justice, mercy and peace in both the Old
and New Testaments. For them this takes priority over other aspects of
God's message when dealing with the Israel/Palestine conflict.

The second is their challenge to Israel's right to be back in the
land. This takes the form of replacement theology. They challenge the
Christian Zionist view of the Abrahamic Covenant and the promise of

the land. For example, like other Covenantalists, Katanacho attempts to make a double metaphor of Ezekiel's Valley of Dry Bones in *Chapter 37*, saying that the resurrection of the Messiah embodies the resurrection of Israel rather than its literal restoration.[7] However, they add another dimension, absent from traditional replacement theology, which is to challenge the identity of the Jews. This is especially true of Raheb and Katanacho. We have already dealt with replacement theology in previous chapters, so in this chapter we will examine the two aspects which differentiate Palestinian liberation theology from traditional replacement theology.

God's justice and mercy

Supporters of Israel do need to reflect on this aspect of the Palestinian case. The Palestinians argue that if Israel has been unjust and oppressive then God will not countenance them being back in the land. It is a variant of the replacement theology argument that Israel needs to repent before it can return to the land.

There is ample Scripture in the Old Testament which expounds God's sense of justice and compassion. He frequently calls upon Israel to demonstrate this, in particular to the widows, the fatherless and the stranger in their midst. The following texts illustrate this:

> *He executes justice for the fatherless and the widow, and loves the sojourner, giving him food and clothing. Love the sojourner, therefore, for you were sojourners in the land of Egypt.*
> *(Deuteronomy 10:18-19)*

> *Learn to do good; seek justice, correct oppression; bring justice to the fatherless, plead the widow's cause.*
> *(Isaiah 1:17)*

> *He has told you, O man, what is good; and what does the Lord require of you but to do justice, and to love kindness, and to walk humbly with your God?*
> *(Micah 6:8)*

It is also possible to demonstrate that Israel's failure to do this was one of several reasons why God exiled them from the land at the time of the Assyrian and Babylonian captivities. The principal reason for this was their practice of idolatry, but their treatment of the poor and vulnerable was high on the list. There came a point where Israel had departed from God's standards so far, and spurned his pleading to return to him, that he finally sanctioned exile, first for the Northern Kingdom and later for the Southern Kingdom as we saw in Chapter 4.

Coming to the present day some anti-Zionists consider that Israel is behaving no better than it did at the time of its first exile; that it is oppressing the Palestinians in the way that it oppressed the weak and vulnerable in its own society.

God's values of justice and compassion are very significant and I do not think that supporters of Israel have always attached sufficient importance to them when considering Israel's dealings with the Palestinians. However, I do not think that they take precedence over his other revelations concerning Israel. I do not consider an appeal to his justice will cause him to hold back his promise to restore the Jews to their ancient land. I offer four reasons for believing this:

1. I argued in Chapter 3 that the return of the Jews is a sovereign purpose of God. I explained that given God's involvement in history this return was unlikely to have been a consequence merely of his discretionary will. God is the God of history as well as creation. For something as major as the return of his people, the Jews, it is unlikely that he would have allowed their return, unless it was his sovereign will to do so.

2. It is also very important to remember that the Arab/Israeli conflict is not a conflict in which all the wrong has been done by one side. It is difficult to avoid the conclusion that some (but not all) Palestinian Christian writers think that the conflict is all Israel's fault. Ateek, while condemning Palestinian violence, always seeks to explain it as a consequence of Israel's behaviour. It is also possible that some Christian Zionists see the conflict as entirely the fault of the surrounding Arab nations and the Palestinian leadership. However, the recent history of the Middle East is hugely complex and whichever side one supports politically, it is

in my view completely unrealistic to hold one side responsible to the exclusion of the other. God is in a position to see the whole conflict. He will know the thoughts and intentions of everyone involved and he will have anticipated strife. He will not judge Israel in a one-sided way.

3. While justice and mercy are very dear to God's heart, it does not encompass the whole of his revelation concerning the Jews. I have attempted to demonstrate that their return to the Holy Land is a major part of his revelation in the Old Testament. Passages from the prophets indicate that a time of justice, peace and cooperation between nations centred on Israel will occur in the future (see *Isaiah 2:2-4; 19:23-25*). Meanwhile we will have to wait for this while God's present purposes are worked out. This is particularly true when we factor into the picture God's spiritual arch-enemy Satan. He does not want peace between Israel and its neighbours and will stir up both sides, Israel as well as the Arabs, to exacerbate the conflict. I will say more about this in the final chapter.

4. The Old Testament revelation demonstrates that God will bring the Jews back to the land *before they repent* and recognise Jesus Christ as their Messiah and Saviour. The Palestinian Christians do not consider Israel to be a fit inheritor of the land. Katanacho echoes the bewilderment of Western Covenantalists who cannot reconcile the restoration of the Jews to their ancient land before they have repented. Katanacho's argument is more specific. He does not mean repentance in a general sense, but refers to what he considers to be their sinful behaviour towards the Palestinians in particular. He says:

> *There is no inheritance without meeting the biblical requirements of justice and righteousness.*[8]

He goes on to specify the Palestinian refugees as the core of Israel's sinful behaviour:

> *Any credible argument for the prophetic place of modern Israel should provide theological justification for the moral state of Israel and for the displacement of hundreds of thousands of Palestinian refugees who lost their homes*

in 1948. These refugees are the people whom God created and loved. Fifty thousand of them were Christians.... Why should God take the Palestinian Church into exile in order to bring a group of people who don't accept Jesus Christ as their Saviour and Lord?[9]

This eloquently catches the sense of grievance the Palestinian Christians feel about Israel, but its eloquence does not make it a valid argument. We will examine the evidence for the return of the Jews before they repent and come to know their Saviour in *Appendix 1, Section 4.*

It is for these reasons that I do not think the argument based on God's justice and compassion, powerful as it may seem, takes precedence over his other revelations concerning the return of the Jews.

The challenge to Jewish identity

This is a subtle attempt to undermine the place of the Jews in God's purpose for humanity. It takes various forms which can be summarized as follows:

◊   Jesus is identified with the Palestinians rather than the Jews.

◊   Many Jews are not Jewish at all. They are Gentile converts.

◊   Intermarriage with Gentiles has diluted Jewishness to the point where the distinction between Jew and Gentile is no longer meaningful.

Before we look at this it is worth reminding the reader that this is an extension to traditional replacement theology. Replacement theology has evolved since its inception in the early years of the Church. Traditionally it always recognised the Jews as Jews. In fact it made a point of highlighting their distinction from Gentiles and in the process castigated them as a people who had rejected their Messiah. In the twentieth century replacement theology softened its approach. It still recognised the Jews as a distinct people, but argued that this distinction no longer served a spiritual purpose. Jews were to be evangelised just like Gentiles and assimilated into the largely Gentile Church.

We now find some Palestinian Christians questioning the very identity of the Jews. Supporters of Israel need to be aware of this. It is a deceptive argument. It shifts the debate from one in which the Jews are not considered to be fit inheritors of the land to one which says that perhaps they are not really Jews at all! If it could be shown that modern day Jews are either not Jewish or that their Jewishness has been so diluted as to be insignificant, then it could be argued that most Jews have no more right to settle in Palestine than any other people. It would then be argued that it is the Palestinians alone who should be considered the historic people of Palestine.

I completely reject this attempt to discount Jewish identity, but because of this challenge I have devoted *Appendix 6, Are the Jews really Jewish?* to this topic. It is a question of ethnicity and I have dealt with it both historically and genetically. Space does not permit me to analyse the arguments of the Palestinian writers, but I would encourage the reader to check out their views in their writings, or the website and references listed in note 10 to this chapter.

Ultimately we can appeal to God on this matter. God himself has kept the Jews apart and ethnically distinct. He was bound to do this since his promise to Abraham was through the ethnic line of Isaac and Jacob. I emphasise once again that the promise was not made to Ishmael or to any of the other sons of Abraham, nor was it made to Esau. Furthermore Jesus was clear in his discourse with the Samaritan woman that salvation comes from the Jews (*John 4:22*).

How ancient are the Palestinians?

In calling into question the genuineness of today's Jews, the Palestinians open themselves up to the same scrutiny. They rightly feel aggrieved that some Westerners dismiss their claims to being a people in Palestine. We should have no reason to doubt that some families can claim a long ancestry in the land, but if they claim ancestry back to the first Christians, how can they be so sure? Without written records tracing their history, how can they be sure these ancestors were not part of the many migrations to and from Palestine in the last 1800 years? This does not mean that the Palestinians do not have a right to live in the land; it is simply being realistic about their possible ancestry.

Conclusion

The Israel/Palestine conflict is about who should live in the land of Palestine. In an ideal world there would not be a dispute about this. There is adequate room for the Palestinian Arabs, the Jews and minority groups such as the Druze.

The Palestinians have a right to live in the land because of an historical association going back many years for some of the families. The Jews have a right to live there because of their ancient association with the land. This book has sought to demonstrate that this association is God given and eternal. It was not a limited or temporal association, even though the Jews were exiled from the land on God's initiative over many centuries.

Both sides in the dispute seek to undermine the other's right to live in the land by questioning their identity as a people or their behaviour towards each other. They have also sought to undermine each other's right by invoking theology. I have sought to show that the Jews right to live in the land cannot be undermined by theology; that the Bible is clear about their inheritance and that God himself has played a part in their restoration.

However, I do think God's requirement for justice can be invoked in relation to how this restoration is achieved. It saddens me to hear supporters of Israel discounting the Palestinians' right to live in the land. Many Palestinians did live in the land before the Jews began to return in 1882. They became anxious with the influx of large numbers of Jews in the 1920s and 30s. Many ordinary Palestinians were uprooted from their homes in 1948.[11] They suffered displacement and bewilderment and this has left a very real legacy of bitterness. However much we support the Jews' right to return to their ancient land, we should always be aware of other people's occupation of this land while the Jews were away from it.

NOTES

1. Wikipedia, *Religion in Israel*. See also Care: <http://www.care.org/careswork/countryprofiles/105.asp>

2. There are also a number of evangelical Arab congregations in Israel itself. They vary in their theological understanding of the restoration of Israel – some support it, while others do not.

3. This threat would be from Palestinians who suspect that a close association with Jews might be evidence that they were informers for Israel.

4. The mainline churches, Catholic and Greek Orthodox, are not sympathetic to evangelical Protestant Christians.

5. Naim Ateek, *A Palestinian Christian Cry for Reconciliation*. P.90-91.

6. World Council of Churches website; search for *Kairos Palestine Document*: <http://www.oikoumene.org/>

7. Yohanna Katanacho, *The Land of Christ, A Palestinian Cry*. P.63.

8. Yohanna Katanacho, *The Land of Christ, A Palestinian Cry*. P.64.

9. Ibid. P.64-65.

10. Naim Ateek, *A Palestinian Christian Cry for Reconciliation*. P.11.

    a. Ibid. P.197. In his note 8 to the preceding passage Ateek qualifies his statement by saying he is using the word Palestinian in a geographic and not an ethnic sense. However, he still does not acknowledge that Jesus was a Jew.

    b. See:<http://www.christatthecheckpoint.com/lectures/Mitri_Raheb.pdf> for the full transcript of his speech. If this is not accessible: Google search: *Mitri Raheb denies Netanyahu is Jewish*.

    c. Yohanna Katanacho, *The Land of Christ, A Palestinian Cry* P.39 through to 65.

11. It is only right to remember that an equal number of Jews were uprooted and expelled from Arab lands during the war of 1948. See Chapter 1, *Israel's challenge to this narrative*.

12 *THE CHURCH'S CALL TO PRAY FOR ISRAEL*

||||||||||||||||||||||||||||| |||||||||||||||||||||||||||||||||||||||||||||||||||||||||||||||||||||||||||||||||||||||||||||||||||||||||||||||||||||

My call from God was specifically to pray for Israel and the Jewish people, so that will be my emphasis in this final chapter. However, the reader will have gathered that I have a lot of sympathy for the plight of the Palestinians and the Palestinian Christians in particular. For this reason I fully respect that other Christians will have been called to pray for the Palestinians, or for particular Arab nations or for Muslims in general. My one reservation is that this should not lead to the political and biblical delegitimisation of Israel. It should be possible to pray for the Palestinians, disapprove of wrongs on both sides and yet still understand that Israel and the Jews are important to God. It is important to remember too that the Jews in Israel have also suffered much at the hands of Palestinian extremists and the surrounding Arab nations.

With Israel's growing unpopularity, some of it self-inflicted, but much of it due to the malevolent intentions of its enemies, many Christians have missed the vital call to pray for the fulfilment of God's purposes for the nation and its people. This is certainly a call to pray for the salvation of individual Jews, but it is more than this. I believe God wants us to pray for the protection of the nation and its people, so that his plans unfold according to his sovereign will. As we shall see, this is a battle in the spiritual realm and Christians are called to play a part in this battle.

In practice the prayer group I lead does not restrict itself to praying for Jews and Jewish believers. We have connections with Palestinian-Arab churches in Israel itself and in the West Bank. It is always a joy to learn about links between Jewish and Arab believers. This is happening on the ground in Israel, as Jewish and Arab fellowships take tentative steps towards each other. This is why I believe it was right, despite their differences, for Messianic Jewish leaders to attend the 2012 *Christ at the Checkpoint* conference at the invitation of the conference organisers. They are brothers and sisters in Christ. With so few Messianic believers and evangelical Palestinian Christians, **surely** God wants them working together and praying together and not to be in discord (*Psalm 133*). This way they can pursue that great work of evangelism: praying for, and witnessing to, unsaved Jews and Palestinians.

The human dimension

I began this book with the experience of a friend who had a dream which revealed the Father's heart for the Jewish people. I have another friend who also experienced a call from God to pray in a similar way. She too was a new Christian and had no idea of the significance of the Jewish people to God. She lived in an isolated place in the country. One night she was praying. It was pitch dark and as she looked at the blackness through her window she had a vision: she saw a train with many wagons from which a long line of people descended and then walked naked into buildings which she recognised as gas chambers. She had lived through the Second World War, so she knew about the death camps. This lasted for some time during which she was impressed with the words: *"Work for his people and give him no rest until he establishes Jerusalem and makes it a praise in the earth."* This friend who was then in her fifties had been a political activist in her former life and thought nothing of phoning her pastor well after midnight! Instead of chiding her, he said: *"I know exactly who you need to speak to,"* and the next day took her to see the leader of the national movement 'Prayer for Israel' who happened to be staying in the neighbourhood.

I have related both these stories because I want to introduce a human dimension. As far as I am able I have dealt with the biblical facts relating to this subject. I have discussed the two main approaches to Israel and the Jewish people which are found among Christians. Shortly, I will return to what the scriptures have to say on the subject of prayer and how it should apply to Israel and the Middle East. But there is a human side. There is a partnership between God and his children. He does talk to us, albeit in ways that are different and much less frequent than normal human communication. For the most part he expects us to walk by faith and discern his will for our lives through prayer and the study of his word, the Bible. Sometimes, however, when he wants to change our direction or introduce us to something new, he speaks more directly and this is what I believe happened to these two friends of mine.

I have met many people who have felt that God has opened their eyes and called them to pray for Israel and the Jewish people. Their stories are not necessarily dramatic, like the two accounts I have related, but they do surprise me with the varied ways God seems to have spoken to them. This is usually the trigger for them to search the scriptures and they always come to the conclusions that constitute the theme of this book. Most of the people I meet are very level-headed in their faith. I know that there are people who 'go over the top' in their enthusiasm for all things Israeli or Jewish and this sometimes discourages their fellow Christians who do not see things in the same way. I have already indicated that I am unhappy with the vogue in end-time Christian literature to try and anticipate in detail what will happen in Israel and the Middle East. It is unwise and may be counter-productive.

The Holocaust

Before I examine the scriptural basis for prayer I wish to relate one other story. I remember one of the leaders of the movement in the United Kingdom which prays for Israel relating a story at a conference. She had friends who had recently visited the death camp at Auschwitz which is now a macabre museum. They were horrified by what they saw and said that one could still sense the presence of evil over the camp. In a time of prayer after the visit one of them said to God: *"How did something so evil ever happen?"* In response she received the words *"Because there was no Esther church!"* Readers will remember that Queen Esther (see the Old Testament Book of *Esther*) was called upon to intercede with the king on behalf of the Jewish people. They were threatened with annihilation in the Medo-Persian Empire. She had a choice and she chose to intercede at risk to her own life.[1]

One could dismiss this as the thoughts of people overaught by the awfulness of what they had just seen. I do not. I believe passionately that God is calling today's Church to recognise the significance of Israel and to start praying for the Jewish people, both individually and as a nation. It is plain for all to see that the Jews in Israel are today under the same existential threat that they were under in the 1930s and the Second World War. With Iranian leaders openly denying the holocaust and declaring that their nation along with others seeks to destroy Israel, this is all too real a threat.[2]

I have recently read a book *Story of a Secret State* by Jan Karski. It is a story about the Polish underground resistance during the Nazi occupation in the Second World War. Karski was a significant resistance leader because he brought definitive and horrifying news to the allied countries of what was happening to Jews both in the Warsaw Ghetto and in the death camps. He was not himself Jewish. Here is what he wrote following a meeting with two Jewish leaders:

> *The first thing that became clear to me as I sat there talking to them in the silence of the darkening Warsaw suburbs was the complete hopelessness of their predicament. For them, for the suffering Polish Jews, this was the end of the world. There was no possible escape for them or their fellows.*[3]

This is what one of the Jewish leaders said to him:

> *'You other Poles are fortunate' he began. 'You are suffering too. Many of you will die, but at least your nation goes on living. After the war Poland will be resurrected. Your cities will be rebuilt and your wounds will slowly heal. From this ocean of tears, pain, rage and humiliation your country will emerge again but the Polish Jews will no longer exist. We will be dead. Hitler will lose his war against the human, the just, and the good, but he will win his war against the Polish Jews. No – it will not be a victory; the Jewish people will be murdered'.*[4]

Karski did not carry this message to the Polish Government in exile through hearsay. These leaders arranged for him not only to visit the Warsaw Ghetto, but actually to gain smuggled entry to the death camp at Belzec, where he saw for himself the killing of the Jews.

The scriptural basis for prayer

I believe today that we are called to be the adopted brother in my friend's dream, but with a change of heart – not to be indifferent to the brother who is in a spiritual coma, but to come alongside the Father and support this brother! What then is the scriptural basis for prayer and in particular prayer for Israel and the Jewish people?

I believe the answer is three-fold:

1. New Testament Scripture demonstrates that Gentile believers are indebted to the Jewish people.
2. God calls us to pray.
3. The reality of satanic opposition in the spiritual realm.

1. THE DEBT

We have already noted the significance of *Romans Chapters 9-11* elsewhere in the book. We will now take a closer look. Here we have a passage in Romans which highlights three things: first, Paul's heartfelt anguish that his fellow Jews might be saved; secondly, that a remnant will be saved; and thirdly, the debt that the Gentiles owe to the Jews as a people. Not only do we obtain salvation through a Jewish Saviour, Jesus Christ, but this salvation appears to be facilitated by what has happened to the Jews.

The metaphor of the olive tree (*Romans Chapter 11*) implies that we, the wild olive branches, are grafted into the Jewish root of the tree. This root still survives despite the fact that many of the natural branches have been broken off through unbelief. This Jewish inheritance sustains us through the sap which feeds the branches. We cannot simply say that we have been grafted into Christ and forget about the Jews. Our acceptance is somehow linked to their temporary rejection as we see from these verses:

I want you to understand this mystery, brothers: a partial
hardening has come upon Israel, until the fullness of the Gentiles
has come in.

(Romans 11:25)

As regards the gospel, they are enemies of God for your sake.
But as regards election, they are beloved for the sake of their
forefathers. For the gifts and the calling of God are irrevocable.

(Romans 11:28-29)

I do not pretend to understand this mystery, but strange as it may
seem they are in some way enemies of God for our sake in the Church
age. We cannot see them as just another ethnic group; their impact is
way beyond that.

2. GOD CALLS US TO PRAY

In Chapter 3 we examined the operation of God's sovereign and
discretionary will. This distinction is essential if we are to allow for the
operation of human free will. Choice also operates in the sphere of
prayer. Most Christians subscribe to the view that Almighty God enacts
many of his purposes in co-operation with his people whom he calls
to pray. I am not suggesting that he only acts in response to prayer,
but the pervasiveness of prayer throughout the Bible suggests that
this is his preferred way of working. This is especially true in the New
Testament. In the Old Testament it tended to be the priests and the
prophets who sought God, but in the New Testament, as the apostle
Peter says, we have all become priests (*1 Peter 2:9*). Once saved we
can all approach God's throne of grace through the blood of Christ
(*Hebrews 10:19-20*).

I believe this is about exercising faith in our walk with God. He
wants our lives to be steeped in prayer (*1 Thessalonians 5:16-18*) and
in some instances he calls people to real intercessory prayer where
they engage with God the Holy Spirit to bring about his desired
changes. But we have a choice. God does not force us to co-operate.
As we have just seen Queen Esther had a choice and she made the
right decision.

Prayer shapes history

Prayer also shapes history. The prophet Daniel was a great intercessor. In *Daniel Chapter 9* we find him humbly beseeching the Lord about fulfilling his promise to Jeremiah. This was the promise that God would restore the Babylonian captives to Jerusalem after seventy years.

Derek Prince was one of the Christian leaders in modern times who brought the Church back to the realisation that through prayer we could influence nations and thus shape history.[5] Older Christians will be aware that King George VI called the nation of Britain to prayer at several critical times during the Second World War. Rees Howells, the famous Welsh intercessor, and his Bible College were called to intercede that the Germans would not break through to the Middle East and capture Palestine.[6]

3. SATANIC OPPOSITION IN THE SPIRITUAL REALM

When we intercede, we engage in a spiritual struggle that is going on, in the heavenly places, between God and his angels on the one hand and Satan and his fallen angels on the other.

This idea is not to every Christian's taste! However, the rise of the Pentecostal churches and the charismatic movement in the twentieth century has brought the Church back to its roots in the New Testament and its activities in the Acts of the Apostles. Much of the Church across the world is now aware that the Christian life is a walk with the Holy Spirit under the lordship of Jesus Christ. Prayer is effective when the Word of God (the Bible) is applied with the guidance of the Holy Spirit. One of the consequences has been to realise that we are in a spiritual battle with the enemies of God led by Satan. Until we are born again of the Spirit of God we are in the wrong kingdom (see *Colossians 1:13* and *1 Peter 2:9 RSV*).

Satan targets the Jews

It was only recently while reading the book by Jan Karski that I learnt that Hitler not only ordered that all Jews should die, but that they must die in agony. Himmler turned the problem over to his advisers who came up with a solution (prior to the gas chambers) which I will not describe. This was not just human depravity, this was satanic depravity.[7]

This brings us very appropriately back to the need to pray for Israel and the Jewish people. Put simply Satan does not like the Jews. They are a constant thorn in his side. They represent God's creation as a race on whom he bestows his love. They represent too the race through whom the Messiah, the Saviour of the human race, would come and eventually did come in the person of Jesus Christ.

Once outside of God's protection the Jews have been persecuted throughout history. This reached its climax in the Nazis 'Final Solution' of the Second World War, Hitler's grotesque attempt utterly to destroy the Jews.[8]

This should give us pause to reflect. Other peoples have been subject to attempts at genocide, but no people have suffered the unremitting hostility experienced by the Jews over so long a period. Today the Jews have their state, the State of Israel. It was born out of the ashes of the war. The guilt of the nations at what had happened to the Jews in this war must have played a part in the decision of the United Nations to sanction this state.

The future of the Jewish state

The nation is strong and the Jewish people will never allow themselves to be unprepared again, but are they safe? In the modern world the concentration of so many people in such a small piece of land makes them an easy target for weapons of modern warfare and mass destruction. If Satan tried to destroy them in the Second World War, then surely it is clear that he will do his utmost now to achieve what he failed to do then?

Whatever is going on in the invisible spiritual realm, it is clear that Israel and the Middle East are at the centre of an intense conflict. The way that the Middle East is seldom out of the news, the seeming insolubility of the conflict and the passions it arouses, all suggest that something unusual is going on behind the scenes.

In the natural Israel is a nation at risk. When we pray for Israel we not only pray for the Jewish people to hear and receive the gospel, we also pray for their survival as a nation.

Why not leave it all to God?

For many years I took this view. It was only when I felt much burdened in my spirit one day and unexpectedly found myself interceding with God that the Church would stand with Israel and the Jewish people that I realised it was important to God. I then sought out people who already felt this way and learnt very quickly that there was a network of Christians both within and outside of Israel who thought likewise. I also learnt that compared with the size of the Church worldwide, this number was very small.[9] I learnt too that there was a major division within the Church, especially in the Western world, between those who felt supportive of Israel and those who did not, which is of course where we started this book!

God does not need us to pray, but he does call us to pray. This is true in the Old Testament as well as the New. In Isaiah (*Isaiah 59:16; 63:5; 62:6-7*) he calls for intercessors and in Ezekiel God tells him that he has made him a watchman for the house of Israel (*Ezekiel 3:16; 33:7*).

Only the Messianic Jews, who are still few in number, seek God through the Person of Jesus Christ. One of the themes of this book is that God is going to reveal himself collectively to the Jews through their Messiah at some point in history. Until they meet Jesus Christ a veil exists over their hearts (*2 Corinthians 3:14-16*); they need our help against both the natural and the spiritual forces that are arrayed against them.

The consequences of not praying

There are consequences to not praying for Israel. We either take the view that what happened to the Jews in the Second World War was ordained by God and nothing could have changed it, or we take the view that prayer could have changed it. Today is similar. In a sober article on the potential nuclear threat from Iran, Shani Sorko-Ram Ferguson has said:

> *I am confident the Jewish people will ultimately survive. But how many Jews will survive is still up for grabs in my mind.*

> *Biblically, the amount of protection Israel enjoys is directly*
> *affected by the amount of prayer that is sent up to heaven by*
> *believers worldwide on her behalf. (See Ezekiel 22:30 and the*
> *Book of Esther).*[10]

This may sound melodramatic, but if it is true then it is clearly right to pray. Either way I would rather God tells me later that I did not need to pray than that I should have prayed!

How then should we pray for Israel?

Given the contentious nature of this subject among Christians it may help if I list first *what is not intended* when we pray for Israel and the Jewish people.

1. It is not to idolise or in any way elevate the nation of Israel and its land above the Person of Jesus Christ. As I have said several times in this book, Jews have to come to salvation just like any other group (*Acts 4:12*).
2. However, it is not simply 'mission to the Jews' as though they were one of many groups to be evangelised.
3. It is not to condone the secular and sinful nature of Israeli society.
4. It is not to take a political or military stand which says that Israel can do no wrong in relation to its neighbours. Israel is a secular nation and most of its leaders do not yet seek God for their nation's future.
5. It is not to argue that Jewish traditions take the place of the essential beliefs of the New Testament gospel.
6. It is not to ask the whole Church, at national or local level, to be equally involved in supporting and praying for Israel.

The essential requirement

The overriding requirement is for the Church to recognise that Israel is central to what God is doing in the world today and that he wants our support. This means public acknowledgement of the Church's support, both at national and local level, and encouragement at local level for individual Christians to set up groups or to join them. These groups can pray for Israel, the Middle East, Arabs and Jews. Church members should be encouraged to ask God whether he wants them to join such a prayer group.

In the United Kingdom in particular, churches at the national level are very quick to pass resolutions which condemn Israel, and even to support academic and material boycotts, and rather slower to indicate that they recognise the significance of Israel in the purposes of God.[11]

At the moment prayer groups are sometimes frowned upon or simply tolerated without any acknowledgement that what they do is an important part of the Church's calling. I meet Christians who feel obliged to leave a church because it is hostile to such groups and they may be asked to disband their group. Of course, I in no way mean to underplay the fact that God gives many tasks to individual churches. In my own church I know people who have a calling to pray for Poland, China and Japan and there will be other people with other countries on their heart.

The call to evangelise the world gets recognition, but the call to pray for and support Israel frequently does not. Recognition and acceptance of this call are the key things required of individual churches and their leaders.

The areas for prayer

How then can individual churches of any group or denomination demonstrate that they support God's purposes in relation to Israel?

1. They can recognise the uniqueness of Israel and the Jewish people in God's purposes for the redemption of the world and, if they wish to, they can include this in their Mission Statement.

2. They can authorise a prayer group for Israel within the church. Not everyone will be called to this work, but church members should be encouraged to discover whether the Lord is calling them to share this burden.

The prayer activity of such groups is likely to cover:

(a) Giving thanks to God for all the Arab, Palestinian and Jewish people who have already come to know Jesus as their Saviour

(b) Petition to God to save Jews in Israel and to increase the number, size and influence of the Messianic fellowships within the nation. It might also include prayer for Jews in the church's home community.

(c) Prayer for Arab, Palestinian and Jewish Christians and for the ongoing work of reconciliation.

(d) Prayer for the protection of Israel and the Jewish people, so that the Holocaust is never repeated.

(e) Prayer for the Government and Authorities in Israel that they will act justly and humanely in the decisions they have to make over the country's security.

(f) Prayer for God to foil the terrorist activities of groups such as Hamas and Hezbollah.

(g) Prayer for God to restrain the hostile activities that occur on both sides between some Jewish settlers and their Palestinian neighbours.

(h) Prayer for the political leaders of other nations. I believe this to be especially important for Britain and the USA, two nations which appear to have been given a special responsibility for the birthing and support of modern-day Israel.

(i) Prayer for God's purposes to be fulfilled for Israel and the Middle East. He does have a plan. It is unwise to try to anticipate it, but we can always pray for its fulfilment. *This enables Christians to agree in prayer where they may have different views on the political solution to the Israeli/Palestinian conflict.*

3. Churches can help finance the work of God in Israel. This is best done by channelling money through the home-grown Messianic and Arab fellowships. The larger fellowships already have efficient means of distributing money to cover the many needs: for example, evangelism and help for poor Arab and Israeli believers (*Romans 15:27*).*

4. They can join with other churches locally and nationally to pray for Israel and the Middle East.

    *A short list of organisations is given in *Appendix 7*, These are charities and are able to distribute money. They usually issue a regular prayer letter or bulletin. In this way both prayer and money can be directed to the needs of Jewish, Arab and Palestinian believers. The money actually reaches Christians this way, and does not find its way into the hands of organisations which may actually be hostile to Messianic believers.

As the reader can see there is plenty to pray about! A group leader needs to keep abreast of what is happening in Israel and the Middle East. There are a number of on-line bulletins from Christian/ Messianic organisations and magazines such as *Israel Today*. These often provide information about what is happening in Israel, that is not easily obtained elsewhere. For up-to-date secular views I find the weekly *Jewish Chronicle* very useful. It is also good to cast a critical eye over our own media (in the UK) where anti-Israel bias easily creeps in. For those to whom this subject is very new, books sympathetic to the theme of this book are marked with an asterisk in the Bibliography (*see the Website*).

Conclusion

Many Christians are aware of the plight of the Palestinians and also of the Palestinian Christians, but how many are aware of the Messianic believers in Israel and the persecution they suffer from some Orthodox Jews? Sadly, the Orthodox Jews see the proclamation of Jesus as the Messiah as a real threat to traditional Judaism. The way some groups persecute certain Messianic congregations can be ugly and dangerous. How many Christians are aware of the growing fellowship between Messianic and Arab fellowships within Israel and to a lesser extent with Palestinian Christians in the West Bank?

When these groups meet there is not necessarily immediate rapport; there may be lively debate, but both sides are working to overcome their differences because they recognise ultimately there will be 'one new man' in Jesus (*Ephesians 2:15*). I hear about this first-hand because our prayer group supports both Jewish and Arab congregations in prayer and in a very modest way financially. The financial support we give through a charity, set up by a retired couple who felt called by God to raise money for needy believers in Israel, Gaza and the West Bank. This is a faith work and is expanding each year. To me this kind of work reveals that God is working behind the scenes, without trumpets or fanfare, to bring people into the kingdom and to unite them once they are in it. Most of the Church in the UK does not hear about this kind of work.

We can influence the politics of the Middle East through prayer, but we can also help to build the united Church of Christ on the ground in the Middle East. I think God takes special delight in this quiet behind the scenes activity of building his Church. We can pray for this as well as God's wider purposes for Israel and the Middle East. That is why we should pray.

NOTES

1. I confirmed that I had heard this story correctly from the leader in question.

2. See Chapter 1, Note 4.

3. Jan Karski, *Story of a Secret State* P.348.

4. Ibid. P.349.

5. Derek Prince, *Shaping History through Prayer and Fasting* Chapter 5. (Part of the larger book: *On Experiencing God's Power* P.371.)

6. Norman Grubb, *Rees Howells Intercessor* P.266.

7. Jan Karski, *Story of a Secret State* Chapter 30 'To Die in Agony ...'

8. Nazis and the Occult, see Chapter 10, Note 1.

9. This is true worldwide, except for the United States where there is a large evangelical body of people who support Israel and the Jewish people.

10. Maoz Israel Report, November 2012: *Israel's Dilemma – To Strike or not to Strike, that is the Question.*

11. A Google Search on the Internet: *Church boycotts of Israel* will give the reader an indication of what has been happening.

SUMMARY OF THE ARGUMENT

The proposition is this: The return of the Jews to the land of Palestine in recent times and the re-establishment of the nation of Israel is in accordance with God's sovereign will and is clearly prophesied in the Bible. The evidence for this is as follows:

1. After an interval of 1700 years during which for the most part the Jews did not return to the Holy Land, they began to return around 1880. This snowballed into the large-scale return that we see today. Given that God is ultimately in charge of history, would he have allowed this return, with all the subsequent turmoil in the Middle East, if it had not been in accordance with his sovereign will?

2. Following the first exile to Babylon there was a limited return to Israel around 500 BC. The bulk of prophecies predicting a return do not fit this limited return from Babylon. Six reasons were given to demonstrate this. The prophecies therefore had in mind a further return which has not happened until recent times.

3. While the Mosaic Covenant was superseded by the New Covenant inaugurated by Jesus, the Abrahamic Covenant was not. The Abrahamic Covenant is eternal and virtually unconditional (circumcision being the only requirement). It promises that Israel will always be a nation before God and will always possess or inherit the land of Canaan.

4. The Mosaic Covenant in contrast indicates that the occupation of the land is conditional on Israel's behaviour, but because of God's

promise to the patriarchs, he will neither utterly destroy the nation of Israel nor permanently exclude them from the land.

5. A nation can only truly be a nation if it has land to occupy. God guarantees that he can allocate this land to a people of his choice, by declaring that the land is his. He puts the seal of ownership on this particular piece of his creation which means that no other nation can lay permanent claim to it, however long they might have occupied the land. They can, however, live there as sojourners or permanent visitors. The clear implication, however, is that they will be subject to Israel's constitution and law. In this contemporary world they could not, for example, vote Israel out of existence or turn the nation into an Islamic state.

6. The importance of Israel being back in the land is to do with God's final reconciliation with the Jewish people and to his faithfulness to his Word. Scripture indicates that God will deal with the nation collectively; yes, they must accept their Messiah, Jesus, as individuals, but on his Second Advent they will meet with him as a nation.

7. There are two avenues open to those who wish to contest this proposition. The first is to argue that the prophecies of a return to the land all fit the limited return from Babylon. This proposition is unsustainable in the face of the evidence. The second is to argue that the Old Testament prophecies about Israel are an allegory for the Church; that by the time of Jesus, the prophecies have been transformed into something different. This argument is seriously flawed for the following reasons:

    (a) God wishes to speak directly to people and has chosen the Bible as his vehicle for doing so. This means that he wishes his message to be clear and to be understood, unless he has deliberately held back its meaning until sometime in the future. Whether God discloses information or hides it he is not ambiguous about it, though he may not disclose the time of its application.

    (b) God does use metaphor and allegory, but in the Old Testament, with rare exceptions, he explains the symbolism so that there can be no confusion in the mind of the reader. This way the reader is not at liberty to make their own interpretation of a metaphor or allegory. (He withheld the meaning of some of the visions given to the prophet Daniel, because they related to the end-times. The prophecies about empires which Daniel was allowed to understand came about as predicted.)

(c) Israel and the Jewish people are always a 'here and now' reality in the Old Testament. God never indicates that the words are to mean something different in the future. It is a belief, without any evidence to support it, that the words Israel, Jew, Land and Jerusalem mean something different by the time we arrive at the New Testament.

(d) The New Testament, while largely silent on the question of the future of the nation of Israel and its occupation of the land, always uses the words Israel and Jew with their ethnic meanings. The one or two instances where this could be questioned in no way warrants a substitution by the word Church.

Summing up, we can say that God's 'cosmic promises' to Israel, the abundant prophecy about the restoration of Israel and God's unbreakable covenant with Abraham, establish this proposition.

POSTSCRIPT

Space has not permitted the inclusion of supplementary material in the published book. The author invites the reader to visit his website; *www.markdunman.com* where this material is displayed as follows:

Appendices

1. Covenantalists' Objections to Christian Zionism
2. Covenantalists under the Spotlight
3. Population Statistics
4. Captivity of Israel and Judah
5. The Second Exile – Did it happen?
6. Are the Jews really Jewish?
7. Support for the poor in Israel, the West Bank and Gaza

Bibliography
Glossary
Historical Timeline
Index of Scripture References
General Index

We hope you enjoyed reading this
New Wine book.
For details of other New Wine books
and a wide range of titles from other
Word and Spirit publishers visit our website:
www.newwineministries.co.uk
or email us at newwine@xalt.co.uk